TALK PIDGIN; SPEAK ENGLISH:
GO LOCAL; GO AMERICAN

TALK PIDGIN; SPEAK ENGLISH:
GO LOCAL; GO AMERICAN

THE JAPANESE IMMIGRANT EXPERIENCE
IN SPRECKELSVILLE, MAUI

WAYNE KIYOSAKI

authorHOUSE®

AuthorHouse™ LLC
1663 Liberty Drive
Bloomington, IN 47403
www.authorhouse.com
Phone: 1-800-839-8640

Published by AuthorHouse 05/05/2014

ISBN: 978-1-4969-0752-3 (sc)
ISBN: 978-1-4969-0750-9 (hc)
ISBN: 978-1-4969-0751-6 (e)

Library of Congress Control Number: 2014907789

In Memory of

Hideki and May Mitsuru Iwanaga Kiyosaki, who gave me life,
disciplined guidance, and unstinting love.

Acknowledgments

Foremost acknowledgment goes to my wife, Jean; son, Mike; and daughter, Miki, for the love, forbearance, and optimism that they provided in helping to guide this book to completion.

A short list of others who provided invaluable knowledge, guidance, and encouragement are, in alphabetical order: Reverend Torako Arine; Alice Yemoto Brooks; Shizuko and Leigh Fukutomi; Stanley Gima; Sara Harrison; Bob and Mary Kiyosaki; Galen Kubota; Robert and Edith Matsumoto; Masako Mera; Warren Nishida; Pearl Horio Nishino; Seiya Ohata; Donald, Jeanette, and Donna Okuda; Clifford Saito; Cherry Sakakida; Terry Shima; Joe Takahashi; June Takano; Tracy and Joan Takano; Lynne Sato Toma; Ted Tsukiyama; Laura Yemoto Wycal; Gladys Wong; Eugene Yamamoto; and Hiroshi Yamauchi.

CHAPTER 1

Prologue

It rained that day, ever so slightly. Misty raindrops, barely perceptible to the naked eye, fluttered down upon my father and me as we gazed in mute sadness at the sugarcane fields that had engulfed the land where our home once stood in Spreckelsville, Maui. We were immersed in "liquid sunshine," an island phenomenon that cast a feathery veil of moisture over us on an otherwise warm and sunny day. It was soon accompanied by a rainbow, a native Hawaiian omen of good fortune, amid which I was reminded that life on Maui, in its full dimension, was about happy memories, and not about the sadness of the moment. It was a welcome back to Spreckelsville and a poignant revelation of time, place, and the guiding values that had always been a part of my life there. It was about a period of life when I was literally swallowed up by the very essence of life as it existed back then and now returned in splendid remembrance to a former state of innocence and unfettered childhood beliefs. In those brief but precious moments, I was transported back to childhood epiphanies that governed my early beliefs about island gods, demigods, ghosts, hobgoblins, and spirits that seemed so real and instrumental in shaping lingering attitudes about fate, faith, and the habitat that was Maui. Those of us who grew up there were children of the soil—a volcanic soil that added an inimitably distinct coloration to all things, animate and inanimate, that influenced our very existence. And it was a personal reaffirmation of a mixture of instinct, emotion, and reason, shaped in accommodation with native logic. In the circumscribed worldview of Spreckelsville, the logic of our thinking was hardly Aristotelian in its reaches. But it was our way of coming to grips with reality.

Thus, on the day of our return to the site of our former home, now returned to earth and reduced to memory like the rest of the adjoining village, I was compelled by intuition and instinct to embrace the moisture that engulfed us as something other than mere rainfall. In my mind's eye, the raindrops were tears, delivered in sad commemoration by the gods and reigning spirits that I long associated with life on the island. The timing was exquisite, especially as I stood next to my father, who, compelled by beliefs long ingrained in his persona, could not allow himself to weep in my presence. He was too stoically Japanese, and I understood. Had my mother, bedridden and too ill to join us that day, been there, she would have wept openly, albeit in the soft, muffled tones so reminiscent of the ways of the women of our old community. As tough and demanding as our parents were in guiding our personal and public behavior, they were not "control freaks," so common to the modern vernacular of behavioral quick fixes. Their iconic contribution to our civic sense of responsibility started on the premise of self-control, which had to be cultivated, not dictated. Without words, they demonstrated through something as simple as their day-to-day behavior that, in the end, we had only ourselves to blame for any failure on our part to live up to the expectations of family, friends, and community.

During childhood, the ultimate sin was to bring shame to family and parents. Our parents would have appreciated the wisdom and soaring implications embedded in the comic wisdom of Pogo, who observed, "We have met the enemy, and it is us." In Trumanesque fashion, they decreed that accountability was personal, and it was to stop at each of our doorsteps. The lifelong lesson also spoke volumes for the moral choices and obligations that they impressed upon us through sacrifices that deferred personal comfort and pleasure for themselves. Parental sacrifice was for the sake of us, their children. In the Buddhist tradition, happiness was to be found in relationships with family, friends, and those around us. It showed us that even poor people could strive for a humble nobility of purpose. It was also their way of inculcating us with patience—a way of sparing us the ravages of instant gratification. Perhaps it was part of the range of sacrifices that a severely restrictive plantation life demanded of everyone. Life translated into long-term goals, not shortcuts. For many of us, we realized all too late in life how much our parents had sacrificed for our sake. We never adequately thanked them. But for them, life was about upholding their responsibilities as parents. Praise was not part of prevailing equations of satisfaction, simply because the demands that they placed on children were not intended to be popular. But in their minds, life's choices were too important to be reduced to popularity contests. Still, they did an amazing job. When an archivist of local lore related a story about a mother who turned the sharing of a can of Vienna Sausage—there was nothing else to eat—into a fun game in which each child received one sausage to go with a meager portion of rice, it struck an immediate and emotionally charged response among the audience. The fact that the mother herself went without eating anything—there were not enough sausages left for her to have any—was not lost on the children. There was no preaching. It was all about homespun teaching wrapped in sacrificial love. No syrupy affectations. No need for morally empty hugs and kisses. It was all about love in undistilled splendor.

That day of return to Old Maui also marked a rediscovery of aloha, a term of both greeting and endearment that expressed our fondest regard and reverence for the people, places, and things that we associated with a Hawaiian diaspora, both real and imagined. For embedded in aloha is the enduring belief in a return to Hawaii, no matter how far one ventures beyond island shores. Thomas Wolfe once reminded us, "You can't go home." But the beckoning of memory has been our way of examining the past to understand who we are and what we stand for. It is part of a Hawaiian heritage, so effectively defined by our parents and peers that turned us into "locals," linked to but not dominated by our ancestry as we became full-blown Americans. It was an evolutionary local identity that was made possible only because of the extraordinary openness of native Hawaiian culture and tradition. We owe a great deal to the native Hawaiians. True Hawaii will live on, as long as local tradition and culture remain intact in the face of swift changes being wrought by the ingress of rampant commercialization. Hopefully, coming generations will allow footprints in the sands of a storied Hawaiian past to sustain shared hopes for a distinct island way of life.

The proverbial stork could not have been kinder in delivering me to Camp Three, where I was born and raised. The stork even had a name. It was Mrs. Yanagi, a midwife of deserved local fame. Some may wonder why I would speak in laudatory terms about a nondescript plantation camp. But to me, it was a place of arresting images and haunting grace, and a place of stark contrasts. For the ordinary plantation family residing there, it was the stage where life was played out, very much like kabuki. Roles, as doled out by fate, demanded a level of emotional self-control that often belied the true state of one's feelings about everyday tasks and obligations. The grinding demands of plantation life and a customary penchant for self-effacement that their Japanese roots demanded were part of a communal identity. Hence, the stereotypical image of people with "no feelings." Just a stoic acceptance of what fate had doled out. Back then, loud individual complaints were regarded as anathema to the stability of close-knit communities. So people endured quietly. *Gaman*, they called it. It meant enduring forbearance. To experience the drama of everyday living in the plantation camps was to gain a starkly intuitive grasp of the galvanizing power that shared emotions represented. Because, underlying a façade of equanimity was a welter of conflicting emotions that only those who lived through them could truly fathom. It is a legacy that remains embedded in our souls. The role that each of us played in that drama became a source of astonishing loyalty to Camp Three. It was a phenomenon replicated in all of the plantation camps of Spreckelsville. Regimentation imposed by a life of hard labor, low pay, and unremitting pressure just to survive and somehow sustain their hopes for a better life was brutal but humanely tolerable because of what the people demanded of themselves. What was intolerable was any attack on the pride and dignity of the people and their way of life. Looks and outward impressions were sometimes deceiving. The people did not represent just a jumble of clichés about coping. It was about accountability to family and community norms. Remarkably, it worked for us.

Central to parental beliefs was a perceived cosmology that linked heaven, earth, and man. Perhaps heaven was unattainable during their earthly existence. But even in abstraction, it was an ideal worth striving for. They looked to *kami-sama*, or a god, in the abstract for salvation. Their constellation of faith was rooted in earthbound phenomena as simple as the soil they cultivated, the water that slaked their thirst and enabled crops to grow, the fire with which they cooked and heated their *ofuro* or communal baths, and the metallic tools such as hoes and cane-cutting knives that defined their terms of labor in the sugarcane fields. All of those life-sustaining activities and encounters with the material world linked them in a very personal way to the cultivation not just of soil and crops but also to the creation of a distinct lifestyle. It was a world of rhythmic sights, sounds, and smells that they unwittingly embraced and welcomed into their definition of soul. What emerged from that very simple linking of heaven, earth, and man was a state of mind—aided and abetted by alchemy, chemistry, myth, and superstition that facilitated the forging of a bulwark of loyalty and devotion to Camp Three.

Camp Three was a kind of place that many would have shunned for its shabby and humble outward image. In outward appearance, it hardly represented an iconic image for stylish living. But somehow the people who lived there were able to discover within themselves simple qualities of unselfishness and a nobility of purpose embedded in those very virtues to sustain not just themselves but also the community as a whole. Writing in the *HAWAII Magazine*, for example, Paul Wood noted that in ceremonies marking the close of the Maui Pineapple Company after one hundred years of operation, sad lament was supplanted instead by "a strong sense of pride" among the old and loyal workers in attendance. Several old-timers were overheard commenting, "we made money in those days."[1] Wood was quick to add that "they didn't mean 'made money' just for their own pockets"; they meant "made money" for the company and the island economy. Indeed, summer work at the cannery helped to pay for the education of many of us. But what was lost on me back then, when I spent my teenage years working at the cannery during summers, was that work, in a very meaningful way, anchored us to the community in which we lived. It was not just a matter of collecting a weekly paycheck. It bonded us to a work ethic that would later prove liberating for all of us.

In college, it made my reading of Max Weber's *Protestant Ethic* all the more meaningful than it would otherwise have been. In hindsight, the hard labor that left me totally exhausted at the end of the workday at the cannery took on a different meaning. Hard labor and the wages that we saved for our education liberated us from the kind of socioeconomic controls that could have dominated our lives. Thus, for those of us who worked there, it was tough to see the company shut its gates. Like the natural beauty of Maui now being eroded by the necessity for modernization and economic rationalization, it meant the loss of part of our heritage.

The contrasts and contradictions embedded in plantation camp life were striking. The first generation was apolitical and culturally conservative. But their children would be driven to more liberal sociopolitical causes. In the gestalt that governed our earliest introduction to socialization, intense pain dictated forbearance instead of desperate outcries. Despair demanded hope. And patience blunted the corrosive threat of quick-fix ideologies. The traditional Japanese explanation for group identity was simple and to the point—the nail that sticks up gets pounded down.

Through it all, individual dignity, even in rare moments of leisure, was framed in faded and sun-bleached mufti, not silken finery. Some joked that one black suit for the men and one silk dress for the women took care of the basic needs to attend all-important marriages and funerals. Life and death were the bookends that framed life for everyone. As they aged, the suits and dresses didn't fit as well. But that was easily understood and overlooked. They were not slaves to fashion in Camp Three. Besides, it obviated a lot of snickering about poor people's appearances at times when the significance of a proper community observance was of greater importance than the look of the clothes they wore.

Labor protests and strikes were not just protests directed to blatant economic inequities. It was as much about the preservation of the identity, pride, and dignity than the notion of equal pay for equal work. It was not just about money, though the money meant a lot to their subsistence lifestyles. For the Japanese immigrants in the camp, a traditional determination to outperform every other group at work appeared hollow when their work was mired in unfair compensation. Fourteen dollars a month as compared to the eighteen dollars a month that other groups were paid was not just unfair. It was demeaning. Humility was not about abject submissiveness. More importantly, the contracts under which they labored appeared to be morally empty of promise. During the early stages of the Vietnam War, an American military officer was moved to comment that the Vietnamese villagers that he observed were "people without feelings." Little did he realize that beneath the stoic image of compliance lay a tradition of seething resentment against foreign intervention that Vietnam had historically endured in its own quest of a national identity. It would eventually undermine our own strategy to "free" and "democratize" the Vietnamese. Self-identity is seldom neutralized by overwhelming military force alone. China, the Mongols of Genghis Khan, France, and more recently America, all cast their own brand of influence on Vietnam. But Vietnam remains quintessentially Vietnamese in its national identity today.

In like fashion, in Camp Three, identity was forged in a crucible of emotional conflict and resolution, sought in genuine pursuit of a better life for future generations. As oppressive as conditions were for them, parents were determined to endure and persevere in defense of their identity. In the hardest of times, they would say, *Nihonjin da mono*, meaning, "after all, we are Japanese," trading on the legacy that "we can endure anything." That was the legacy of sacrifice that our parents bequeathed to us. Not just through empty rhetoric, but through real-life examples of perseverance under duress. And in that process the importance of "we" as a family was solidified as a vital part of family and community unity

The fits and starts that marked the start of this book were initially frustrated by shaky assumptions and loose frames of reference. My problems were also compounded by memories too deeply immersed in consciousness to facilitate immediate recognition and expression of their significance. It was a problem similarly encountered by relatives and friends who helped me to recall past memories. Yet, with each daunting challenge, frustration somehow morphed into joy, occasioned by the chase to recapture parts of a nostalgic past. It ceased being a Sisyphean quest. The slippery slope gradually yielded traction. "Talk story," the local Hawaiian version of oral history, became my link to a storied past that relatives, old friends, and classmates were only too willing to share.

In the process, I also realized the significance that pidgin English played in bridging the early generational and ethnic divides of Hawaii's polyglot society. Pidgin English facilitated communication between native Hawaiian, Chinese, Japanese, Korean, Filipino, Portuguese, and various European immigrants as they embraced English as their primary language even as they remained unavoidably tied to their own native tongues upon landing in Hawaii. Besides, segregation by ethnic groups, as plantation policy, was supposed to have provided a convenient hedge against assumed threats of organized labor activities. On the other hand, the sugar planters had invested heavily to bring overseas labor into the islands to work the fields. It was to their interest to recoup their investment in hopes that the first generation of immigrant laborers would also provide a second generation of laborers for their plantations. The greater the gulf in communication between the ethnic groups, the better it would be for the maintenance of a stable pool of labor. Pidgin English was and still remains a badge of identity among locals. Most of us realized that a command of standard English was the way to integration and success in American society, but like comfort food, the lure of pidgin has always remained persistent. No matter where I travel in this world, it is the one thing that allows me, and other locals like me, to identify a fellow Hawaiian. It is in the tradition of that era that I have pursued this study. I leave it to scholars far more qualified than I am to bring an academic rigor to the study that Spreckelsville deserves.

The ultimate reward in writing this story came when it turned into a labor of love. For those of us who were involved in pooling our memories, it made us even more aware of who we are and how we tend to define ourselves. The fits and starts that marked the journey into this story embraced the wisdom of an ancient Chinese proverb: "A journey of a thousand miles must begin with a single step."

Hesitancy eventually succumbed to optimism. Perhaps some of the optimism was unwarranted. But life in Spreckelsville was based on the belief that better times lay ahead, even under unlikely circumstances. Good times have indeed come to pass for many of us, and that in itself has provided the goad to this audacious look back in nostalgia and memory to a life that was decidedly worth living—an American experience with local Hawaiian flavor. Former House speaker Tip O'Neal had it right when he said, "All politics is local."

CHAPTER 2

The Legacy of Claus Spreckels (1828-1908)

To know how to dissemble is the knowledge of kings.

—Cardinal Richelieu, *Mirame* (circa 1625)

Spreckelsville derived its name from Claus Spreckels, an émigré, born on July 9, 1828, in Lamstedt, Germany. Fate brought Spreckels, in eponymous linkage, to a stretch of land on Maui that continues to honor his legacy in name. In rough outline, Spreckelsville's line of demarcation stretches from the shoreline bordering Kahului Airport to the area of Lower Paia, and then up toward Pukalani before skirting past Puunene, in a curving pattern back to the edge of the airport. Aside from a street previously named in his honor in Honolulu where his home once stood in the vicinity of Punahou, it is probably the only reminder of his legacy in Hawaii. In some quarters, it is a legacy etched in controversy. In others, he is remembered as a man who energized the growth of the sugar industry in Hawaii with unprecedented vigor—particularly on Maui. Despite the personal predilections attributed to his persona, both favorable and unfavorable, the fact remains that "Dee Boss," as he was derisively referred to in some quarters, undoubtedly carved a memorable niche on Maui. His relatively short reign as the "sugar king" of Hawaii was marked by a series of signal achievements. His recognition as "king" was not bestowed gratuitously. He clawed his way to success. In his own defense, Claus Spreckels could likely have averred that he rightfully "earned it." How he earned it was not open to conjecture among those of us who were born and raised in Spreckelsville. He appeared on Maui way before our generation's time.

Life in America began for Spreckels as an employee of a green grocer. He had barely emerged from childhood by then. As a mark of his early determination to succeed in America, he had already carved a niche for himself in the sugar refinery industry in California by the time he arrived in

Hawaii on August 14, 1876. He was forty-eight years of age. His mission, as the leader of the California delegation of sugar refiners, was to deliver a formal protest against passage of a US-Hawaii Reciprocity Treaty that threatened to lower the competitive market price of their products on the mainland.

Ironically, and unbeknownst to him, the treaty had already been ratified in Washington prior to his departure for Honolulu, and the message of its passage was in fact being delivered on the very ship that was transporting him to Hawaii! Surprised but undaunted by the unexpected turn of events, Spreckels turned the setback into opportunity by exploiting a whole new range of possibilities that he saw evolving in the Hawaiian sugar industry. Without hesitation, he plunged into the fray already joined by powerful inside and outside interests to gain dominance in the Hawaiian sugar industry. The rest is history.

As early settlers of the plantation camps of Spreckelsville, the first generation of contract laborers was hardly cognizant or even inclined to judge how Spreckels came by his achievements. Truth be told, they didn't even know who he was. But the very fact that Spreckelsville was named after him, made him, ipso facto, an *erai hito*, or great man, in the feudal-inspired thinking of the first generation Japanese settlers. That was good enough for them.

Had the likeness of the man been captured in stone or cast in bronze, we would have had some inkling about the physical dimensions of a man whose actions cut a wide swath through the political, economic, and social landscape of Maui during his relatively brief presence on the island. Nor was he memorialized in the lore of the locals. Truth is, in blissful ignorance, we chose to embrace the legacy of the place rather than the man. No offense meant against Spreckels himself. We were "provincials" and "county jacks" with views of the outside world that seldom strayed beyond the shoals of Maui.

Undoubtedly, however, the string of achievements that he has left as his legacy firmly attests to his skill and drive as an entrepreneur.

Born dirt-poor, with little if any formal education, he nevertheless parlayed a natural acumen for business into untold wealth and influence—first on the mainland and then in the islands. There are indications that a certain amount of boorishness and lack of social grace as defined by prevailing New England missionary standards may have impeded his acceptance into local social circles. But there are also indications he was no shrinking violet, and in the smoke-filled salons of Hawaiian monarchical society, where cigars and free-flowing alcoholic beverages stoked the never-ending quest of coveted "deals," a capacity for dissembling and cunning served Spreckels well in his relations with well-placed "friends" and business adversaries alike.

In his book *The Water of Kane*, O. A. Bushnell, a noted and insightful chronicler of island life and lore, quotes an archival source as saying that Claus Spreckels was a "short, squat, and pudgy" individual with a penchant for "crusty, arrogant and demanding" behavior.[2] The descriptor appears credible for someone who arrived on Hawaiian shores as an "outsider'" and latecomer, faced with daunting odds against successful entry into Hawaiian society. One can also imagine the undisguised hostility and resentment that greeted his entry into the wanton, frontier atmosphere of commerce that was beginning to take shape in the Hawaiian Kingdom. But like the immigrant workers of lesser intent and hope who followed in the wake of his achievements into citizenry, he, in good measure, persevered successfully in clawing his way to access and eventual acceptance (perhaps even grudgingly) in Hawaii.

Unwittingly, his legacy of success also became a significant part of our own legacy of identity. As immigrants, we dotted the landscape with ethnically distinct faces and with correspondingly varied cultural tendencies. But ultimately we were left to shape our own fate. And in that encounter with fate, the legacy of traditional culture and of our identification with that tradition enabled us to survive and prosper in our own little way, just as Spreckels prospered in a big way in Spreckelsville. Spreckelsville became our *furusato*, our hometown.

I left Spreckelsville soon after graduating from high school. College, military service, graduate school, gainful employment, and marriage led to settlement in the vicinity of the nation's capitol. Yet, Spreckelsville has always been "home" to me. Over the years, recollections of the place and its founder have taken many turns. One such recollection stands out.

During a post-Cold War visit to St. Petersburg, I was stunned to see a broken statue of Lenin lying in ignominy at a dump site in the city that once bore his name. It was a stark reminder of a storied national past trumping revolutionary excess. As I wandered about, examining other relics of a violent revolutionary past, to my surprise, I was approached by our Russian tour guide. Dressed as she was in simple, unflattering garb, unsmiling and effecting a dour countenance, her outward demeanor did little to invite casual conversation with her. She always appeared standoffish. Throughout her brief presence as our local tour guide, she presided over her duties with stern efficiency and businesslike aplomb. Prior to her arrival at my side, as I wandered about the grounds in silence, the only distraction came when, to my utter astonishment, I spotted someone from our tour group surreptitiously handing out copies of the Bible to excited panhandlers who didn't seem to know what they were getting from her. Close by, another member of our tour group gleefully handed out American souvenir ballpoint pens. She returned to the group, glowing until she discovered that one of the children surrounding her had stolen her wallet. Suddenly, well-intentioned moral purpose turned into a brief moment of gnawing cynicism for her.

Through all of this, to my surprise, our tour guide had remained by my side. She then asked me where I was from. I told her that I was born and raised in Hawaii and that my parents were originally from Japan. She then went on to tell me that she was a mere toddler when the German army surrounded the city during the siege of Leningrad that lasted for some nine hundred days doing World War II. Still betraying no emotion, she described how they were completely isolated and reduced to ever worsening stages of starvation. They foraged for grass and anything that appeared even remotely edible. Then, she said, one day, miraculously and out of nowhere, people arrived with fresh loaves of bread to feed the starving children. The bread, she said, was indescribably delicious, matched only by the genuine love and compassion extended to the starving children by adults who quickly faded into anonymity, never to be seen again by the children. She stressed that the experience left her with an indelible image of genuine charity, and it was something that she would cherish as long as she lives. Then she added, "The people that gave us life and hope looked just like you." They were apparently Kazakhs of Asian descent. Somehow, her description of her Asian-looking benefactors made me think of the women of Spreckelsville, who except for the fact that they were Japanese rather than Russian, reminded me so greatly of our guide.

I wanted to continue our brief conversation, but it was time to board the bus to get to our next destination. As she turned to assume her duties as our tour guide, I detected a trace of a smile on her face for the first time, and there appeared to be tears forming in her eyes. It was a strikingly emotional experience for both of us.

We were from two vastly different cultures. Yet, in one brief moment we bonded across racial and cultural boundaries very much unlike the misbegotten attempts at charity that we had just witnessed. There in St. Petersburg, I was restored to faith in the wisdom of an ordinary person of no special claim to moral authority who described an act of spontaneous love and charity to me in a way that somehow made me appreciate the roots of a heritage that was first shaped in Spreckelsville. For me, it was a memorable return to a renewed sense of humanity.

And then, Lenin's broken statue was lying there, a testament to the fickleness of politics and bent ideological formulations that contributed to the undermining of his own legacy.

There are no statues, broken or unbroken, of Claus Spreckels on Maui. He exists only in name. But what he gave to Spreckelsville was a legacy that continues to give name to our own landed identity.

Claus Spreckels, a European by birth, probably did not typically embody the ideals of the European Enlightenment. But he was a product of the forces that shaped the web of ideas that the Enlightenment produced. Like the poor immigrants of Spreckelsville, he, out of necessity, confronted life philosophically without any grounding in classical philosophic thought. He became a pragmatist of pronounced capitalist leaning who eschewed peasant life to turn himself into an idealist, which earned him both riches and notoriety. In the turbulent competitive environment in which he operated, greed, common in those days in varying degrees, was a major goad to his success. Pronounced bouts with deprivation since birth apparently fueled his determined quest of wealth. But in the end, he himself was undermined by the greed of his own sons. Like so many others, he was eventually undone by generational differences in his own family. It was also a reminder that the revolutionary changes wrought in Spreckelsville in capitalistic endeavor did not suffer from the kind of ideological upheavals that still roils over troubled countries in other parts of the world today. The broken statue of Lenin serves as a reminder of that. On the other hand, Claus Sreckels, as a man of decidedly lesser political ambition, reminds us that he gave us a good place to live, work, and grow, and that although life in the plantation camps was no bed of roses, it allowed a stable bedrock of human charity to become part of our lives. The experience in St. Petersburg put all of that in new light; at least, it did for me.

Life in the early days of plantation life in Spreckelsville was difficult for new immigrants. There was virtually free housing, firewood, kerosene, a modicum of health care for emergencies (a standard plantation joke: you go to the dispensary to get treated; you go to the hospital to die), plus other necessities provided for all workers to compensate for low wages. The plantations also had to cope with profit margins to survive. Soon enough, it became apparent to parents that the "good life" was not within easy reach, particularly at $14 a month for six days of labor per week. Margins for survival were just too tight even to allow for much-sought-after savings. Claus Spreckels would never have abided such conditions for himself. When the Japanese immigrants learned that their wages were lower than those of the European immigrant workers, it sowed the first seeds of labor discontent. But the concept of strikes that first emerged in early Japan took on a different slant than in the West. In her book, Ruth Benedict once observed, "Strikes in Japan today have many parallels to the old Peasants' Revolt where the farmers' plea was always that the taxes and corvees to which they were subject interfered with adequate production. They were not class warfare in the Western sense, and they were not an attempt to change the system itself." In hindsight, there appears to have been some of that way of thinking present among the first generation of immigrants, who saw the inequality of wages to productivity as an assault on their traditionally ingrained pride as productive people.

The bonding between land, people, and community that eventually evolved in Spreckelsville was taut and beyond easy dissembling. Poverty and social discrimination made the first generation of immigrants look inward to their heritage for survival and hope. It kindled a sense of identity to rely on, and, in the ensuing process, they discovered a renewed sense of self-worth in who they were and what they stood for instead of succumbing to despair. Struggle against adversity became a source of intense pride. They hunkered down, with few, if any, public displays of belligerence toward anything or anyone around them. Meanwhile, individual liberty could be deferred, contingent on the eventual arrival of constitutionally guaranteed rights for their American-born children.

The physical accommodations offered by camp life were Spartan, to be sure, but that was a different era—an era of ingrained beliefs about social classes and divine missions. *Shikata ga nai* (that's life) was the usual response of the first generation of Japanese immigrants. Life was about moving on in hopes of achieving a better future, with few, if any, guarantees of success. Life was a gamble, and their mantra was in the spirit of "Go for broke," or "Shoot the works!"

There are indications of late that embedded in the American mission in Asia was a veiled agenda, attributed to powerful figures at the highest reaches of government in Washington, to turn the American annexation of the Philippines and Hawaii into opportunities to establish forward bases for access to the lucrative China trade and, in addition, to extend the white Protestant Christian mission to tame and civilize the "backward" peoples and cultures of the East. Many of us, like me, who became Protestants committed to Christianity without ever being aware of the secular implications of religious conversion. We thought it was only about religion—no more, no less. Unlike the threat of European colonization of which the American leadership had to be aware, we were unaware of the fervor of the messianic Christian missionary movement that was destined to transform life in the Hawaiian Kingdom. It is probably safe to assume that Claus Spreckels's priorities were more personal.

In hindsight, the popular notion that the missionaries came to Hawaii "to do good but did well instead" deserves some expansion. There is no doubt in the minds of many locals that some of the early missionaries were often excessively demanding and overbearing in their attitude and conduct toward the native Hawaiians. The plantation system was dogged by systemic limitations that allowed many individuals to exploit the system for their own needs, particularly at the midmanagement level. This included many Southern European immigrants who also arrived in Hawaii as immigrants. Without being dismissive of the excesses of that period, it has to be recognized that it was that kind of period in history when "crusades" of varying stripes were similarly occurring in other parts of the world. It may not have been right, but it was a time of "might makes right." It was a harsh and demanding environment for political and religious conversion.

But by natural selection, the first generation of missionaries gave way eventually to a second generation of men such as H. P. Baldwin and Samuel Alexander, scions of the sugar industry in Hawaii, who, unlike their forbearers, were locally born. They too were locals but of a different kind. They also bore the onus of being regarded as elitists raised in cradles of plantation privilege, which was not necessarily an advantage in their expansion of self-image. They too had to cope locally for influence. As New World challenges evolved in various guises, children on both sides of the tracks—rich and poor—would produce generations of men and women who could not or would not measure up to the expectations of their parents. But on a positive note, it introduced a process of creative accommodation on both sides that subtly abetted a new era of management-labor relations. In near imperceptible ways, it also engendered a narrowing of class divisions.

My father had been commissioned on many occasions to photographically capture ongoing operations in the sugarcane fields of Maui. At one of the annual folk festival exhibits sponsored by the Smithsonian Institution on the capital mall in Washington, DC, a few years ago, which featured the state of Hawaii, I was thrilled to find that most of the photos depicting sugarcane operations were credited to my father. Scenes depicted both *lunas*, or field bosses and workers framed in labor, but never in the conceit of feigned social integration. Reality was framed in the integration of operational responsibilities.

Claus Spreckels never became a local. His presence in the islands was comparatively short. His successors; namely the men from the Big Five, grew up with roots in the islands. The meaning of "*haole*" (white) began to take on new meaning. Social distinctions remained, but they were less pronounced. The children of missionaries were locals, and their preoccupation was not messianic religious conversion. They sought commercial growth and profitability for a sugar industry plagued by lagging productivity, old technology, limited capitalization, and the lack of stable sources of labor. Doing good meant abiding by the rules of secular economics. They too faced formidable competitive pressures from outsiders such as Spreckels.

Like the earlier experience of other developed countries in Europe and Asia, the fundamental problem impeding the expansion of the Hawaiian sugar industry was the lack of stable sources of water. Prior to that, what was to become the future locale of Spreckelsville was barren land. Natives viewed the barren land for what it was. What the new breed of *haole* entrepreneurs, both insiders and outsiders alike, envisioned that native purveyors of subsistence agriculture did not, was the enormous advantage that an integrated irrigation system could bring to agricultural production on Maui. Having emerged from a rice paddy culture, the Japanese immigrants had no trouble seeing the efficacy of, and adapting to, a new form of irrigation system—a system that would ultimately lead to the greening of a once-barren countryside and the founding of Spreckelsville.

The solution was simple enough. But the obstacles were mammoth. Water, cascading down from the tropical rain forests of East Maui, had to be harnessed to feed into the parched lands of Central Maui instead of cascading into the Pacific Ocean. Essential engineering equipment was lacking, and in most cases was nonexistent. Native taboos against the desecration of the land existed all along the way just to lay down pipelines. And the ecology of an ancient volcanic landscape demanded careful unprecedented steps all along the way.

The first and perhaps arguably most significant breakthrough in harnessing the water supply came through the visionary efforts of missionary descendants Henry Perrin Baldwin and Samuel Alexander. Both were local Punahou High School graduates whose basic knowledge of physics allowed them to visualize the construction of the path-breaking Hamakua ditch in upcountry Maui. How they endured in the face of shaky financing, which men like Claus Spreckels could have surmounted with mainland financing had they faltered, how they handled inordinate technical problems, overlaid with local superstitions that threatened access, plus the shaky availability of qualified labor are now part of the trove of local legend.

A seminal effect of the irrigation project was the vital underlying impact that it had on island culture. Casts of wandering European mercenaries and even brigands in search of opportunities brought a unique blend of needed technical skills to the project. Add to that the presence of selected Japanese immigrants who discovered unforeseen opportunities to apply their skills to something other than ordinary physical labor, with aid from friendly Chinese men who, with skill and imagination, provided daily provisions and overall logistical support for the crew under trying conditions. While China and Japan remained at loggerheads over nationalistic issues, there occurred on a small island in the Pacific a process of amity and cooperation between poor and humble immigrants from both countries who saw fit to work together instead of fighting and loathing each other on Maui. The more experienced Chinese on the irrigation project provided indispensable guidance for the Japanese immigrants on matters as basic as local customs and beliefs that also abetted their acculturation to Hawaiian ways.

According to A. O. Bushnell, it ushered in an era in which the early Japanese immigrants began to forsake Japanese ways for local Hawaiian ways. Like the Chinese, intermarriage with Hawaiian women ensued for many lonely Japanese bachelors. It provided a way out of cramped isolated life in hastily erected barracks, into local Hawaiian society. Moreover, unlike the highly structured ways in which relationships were defined for them in Japan, there was a spontaneity that governed their relationship with the local Hawaiian women. Even more significantly, a positive relationship of trust and respect began to evolve between the *haole* bosses and the handpicked coterie of Japanese artisans with whom they cooperated to solve myriads of mounting engineering problems. The ecology that they encountered on the slopes of Mount Haleakala was daunting. Millions of years in the making, the volcanic soil that erupted from the ocean floor produced a shape and mix of natural and cosmic challenges. The mix of human intelligence and practical skill that each side brought to a joint effort to tame nature was vital to the solution of unremitting problems. Soil stability, ravines, gulches, and myriads of problems associated with the land dogged their efforts every inch of the way. And from their remarkable success in building the Hamakua ditch, there emerged a cosmic shift in the sociopolitical milieu of the island. The simple expedient of mutual need and pronounced substantive appreciation on both sides produced an unexpected amelioration of hard-core, class-based ideology and the emergence of glimmers of democratic thought yet to be articulated among locals. To be sure, watercress sandwiches for the *haoles* would not immediately replace *ochazuke* (hot tea poured over a bowl of cold rice garnished with pickles) for the Japanese as midday repasts, but an understandable appreciation of local tastes began to emerge. The *haoles* began to comprehend pidgin English and became unwitting progenitors of a local culture themselves. The flow of water that gushed forth from the Hamakua ditch ultimately energized the economic growth of Spreckelsville. We had our own version of a "hydraulic culture" to transmit local culture.

Efflorescence replaced barrenness as men and soil conspired to produce a miracle of growth that transformed the Central Maui countryside. Upon that welcoming soil, we "walked the walk and talked the talk" as locals, not in lockstep or full equality, of course, but most importantly, toward civic maturity. The symbolic reach across class and racial lines was never given to ostentatious gestures within the Japanese immigrant community. By nature (in backhanded thanks to the Tokugawa feudal legacy) the Japanese immigrants in particular were not "touchy-feely" people. To put it crudely, and very much unlike the new generations, they "knew their place" and instinctively respected higher authority.

The following encounter was emblematic of the evolving social climate. The setting is a dark assembly point in Spreckelsville, where both men and women gather to be transported for a day's labor. That way, work commences when it is still cool, minimizing the time that they will have to work in the blazing heat of day. A car pulls up, and a *haole* boss steps out to watch the loading of the trucks to transport the workers to the fields. At that time of the morning, it is cold, and darkness adds to the somber mood of everyone. A voice breaks the silence:

Goot moruning Mis-tah Kling-Kling! [sic]

Not the sun, not the moon, not the sky!

Ay Toshio, the boss replies, plenty work today eh?

Mochiron! (of course), we make pu-renty hana-hana! (work)

(Good hearted laughter ensues)

The exchange in banter between the two men became a source of derision among the kids in Camp Three. They laughed hilariously about the hopelessly obtuse statement about "not the sun, not the moon, not the sky." Their laughter also betrayed a sense of embarrassment about the older generation's English usage. What the youngsters did not realize was that the importance of what was said was not about proper English usage or misplaced poetic license. It was about bridging the linguistic and cultural divide through such empathetic gestures of goodwill. Nothing more, nothing less intended. In such exchanges both boss and worker understood what was intended. It also exemplified another step toward pidgin language and culture in the making for the boss as well as for the worker. We, as uncomprehending kids, were the ignorant ones, because in such casual banter between boss and worker, barriers of "invisibility" that rigid class stereotypes cause begin to evaporate. Each side began to see individuals for what they were rather than what they thought they were. It placed social class inequities and privileges in a more humane light.

In hindsight, even a remote hint of democratic ideals was preferable to growing up under rigid ideological political systems that stifle and plague human quests for individual self-realization and redemption elsewhere in the world. European immigrants had it right when they stared in awe at the Statue of Liberty. In Hawaii, we were part of a process of lurching democracy, of which we knew little. But we had longings as well, and that, in the long run, preserved our faith in the promises of liberty and justice. Evolving academic awareness made us realize that history does not evolve on greased skids. Buried in that awareness (enforced by concerned parents) was the traditional Japanese penchant for orderly and self-aware progression, despite the impatience of younger generations.

If Thomas Jefferson had been allowed to share a mythical perch with John Locke, the eminent English political philosopher—to whom he owed much of the ideas expressed in the American Declaration of Independence—together, they could have peered down on the evolving plantation life of Spreckelsville, as a place bereft of the conventional ideals of "life, liberty, and the pursuit of happiness." Just as the soaring principles articulated by Locke and Jefferson became a work in progress in Colonial America, it was also a work in progress in Spreckelsville, especially for Asians. The anti-Chinese immigration act of 1882 and the anti-Asian act of 1924 posed severe constraints on the lives of the first generation of Asian immigrants. Self-realization would take a great deal longer to wend its way to us. But it was destined to arrive eventually. We were counseled by our grandparents, who emphasized that good things come to those who wait. Fate was not disposed to prompting by mere mortals, and they made it clear that we were the merest of mortals. Prepare for whatever comes our way; good or bad, they said. Meanwhile seek redemption in self-help. To which my father added that in the twenty-fours a day that life allows us, the ideal is to spend eight hours at work, eight hours at play, and eight hours at rest—all to be pursued with gusto—not just for personal growth but for a common weal that we had yet to fully understand. Translation: discipline starts with structure, which we, as children, were initially not thrilled to hear. My father seldom said much, but when he spoke in earnest, we listened. For us, seemingly primitive aphorisms, delivered in short bursts, led to higher ideals. And it worked out, finally, with statehood, and that too is now part of our legacy—an American legacy with local accent.

For many of us, what Spreckels bequeathed us was a mixed plate of significant remembrance because of the positive melding of good and bad that shaped our collective conscience. The mixed plate lunches that we will savor forever were not only remote forerunners of modern fusion cuisine. They represented a metaphor of local integration that we digested through a "foodie's" appreciation of diversity. Through natural progression, the idea of integration traveled from the stomach to the heart. Back then, we couldn't imagine *haoles* eating raw fish and sushi, but they did. Through the interactive dynamic of yin and yang—positive and negative polarities integral to Chinese philosophical thought—we discovered a shirtsleeve expression of integration. How we learned to view past physical and emotional struggles, in perverse ways, contributed to our growth as committed local citizens. For immigrant parents, unremitting hardship, which they seem to have accepted as a natural part of immigrant progression in the new world, visibly sparked perseverance as a vital source of self-realization. They thereby helped to negate the corrosions of envy, resentment, and quick-fix solutions as answers to our social problems. They themselves could have wallowed in despair, grief, and envy. Instead, their belief in self-reliance proved crucial to the shaping of our identity and indeed to a fundamental understanding of democracy as one of the most difficult forms of governance to implement, even in the modern world. That too had to be earned and not given to us. It was about the inculcation of homespun pride. They didn't demand Japanese translations or translators to make their way into American life. They made do with pidgin English and dirt-stained displays of common sense. There was still a fundamental linkage between the moral order and the social order tied to family values that was defining local culture. The counterculture of the '60s lay way in the future.

Great monuments, as we were taught, are supposed to radiate knowledge and higher human ideals. Some stand in mute testimony to landmark achievers and achievements but are not widely inclusive and therefore prone to empty symbolism. Too often, politics and sheer neglect trump social conscience. Nor do they voice ideals for effect. They are not transportable, except through the medium of human consciousness. There are no physically imposing monuments for those who are humbled by circumstantial life, as our parents were. Their legacy was to make us look inward, to test our mettle and not to seek redemption by blaming others or society at large. To do so was to ignore the challenges posed by fate, as the cornerstone of personal redemption. We were unknowingly blessed, because our monument to the Spreckelsville of yore became a monument in celebratory memory, where it has counted most.

Memories are inevitably fragile, but they persist, even in faded state, in linking us to a storied past. The lore of Spreckelsville is about sources of identity and the culture that sustained it. It is about a bank of memories, tarnished in spots by modern-day erosions inevitably wrought by mindless pursuits of material aggrandizement and tawdry status symbols that detract as much as they attract us. We were as ordinary and as vulnerable as the trends that engulfed us. We were unburdened of old thoughts in ways other than the ways in which our parents had been burdened by them. Instead, they served us new tea in old teapots. Modernity allowed new generations to divest themselves of Confucian dictums such as "to profit is to err," particularly when financial gain was perceived to have been begotten at the expense of more unfortunate human beings. In the new "dog-eat-dog" world of commerce, neo-Confucian thought had to be unshackled from traditional Confucianism. In that regard, the experience of the Chinese immigrants in Hawaii was instructive. We could see how the Chinese immigrants earned their freedom by becoming successful business investors while early Japanese immigrants initially plodded along as savers. There was a healthy trace of Claus Spreckels in the thinking of the Chinese immigrants. Confucius may have been born over twenty-five hundred years ago, but he too had a subliminal impact on our lives as practical philosophy, not as religion, as some were prone to regard his philosophy. It was a sign of the times that China itself would embrace in revolutionary takeover.

As much as Spreckelsville was about the brilliance, drive, and foresight that captains of the sugar industry brought to Maui, beginning with Claus Spreckels, it is also about those who toiled in the fields. As tillers of the soil, the immigrants were economically poor but blessedly steeped in the virtues of rich native cultures. Old virtues also begot faults, but the sheer need for integration into a new world order led to modified adjustments to reality. Old cultures sustained a bedrock of values that enabled the people to persevere in humility, not in humiliation. Some may wonder whether the sheer diversity in ethnicity and cultures, as extant features of plantation life, contributed to a form of accommodation within Spreckelsville. "Divide and conquer," if intended, could possibly have fostered submissiveness to plantation life. In the end, humanitarian values seemed to have spawned a muted sense of purpose, devoid of overriding resentment. It led to shared efforts to level the uneven playing fields that confronted immigrant entry into plantation society. Shared interest energized, in various ways, a communal, nonideological determination to help each other to succeed in an unfamiliar new world. It was not about bearing gifts. It was about giving of themselves to positive beliefs. Problems were shared problems that stirred common emotions. That was the value of the sense of community that evolved spontaneously in places such as Spreckelsville. Unwittingly, it also spawned a unique local culture that thrived in a very tiny but vital enclave of American life. Back then, Hawaii was not an American state. It was the Territory of Hawaii, where the imprint of Claus Spreckels was first established.

The subenclaves of Spreckelsville were segregated plantation camps. Ethnic segregation, we later learned, was ostensibly designed to allay worries about the threat of organized labor movements cutting across ethnic lines. Keeping mothers barefoot, pregnant, and down on the farm, joined by nineteenth-century notions about "divide and conquer" as arcane methods to stabilize labor markets was hardly startling to old-world immigrants who themselves were seeking to escape the restrictions of old-world values. It was like, "So what else is new?" For a new generation, it would make economics and politics first orders of the day once the challenges of survival were overcome. In the process, a fine line evolved between economic determinism and sociopolitical necessity. Ultimately, moderation ruled the day, pending the arrival of modern trade unionism (of which we knew very little as kids) to the islands. Meanwhile *gaman* defined the necessity for perseverance.

In an informal lecture recorded at a local Buddhist discussion group, an invited guest, who just happened to be a baptized Christian, talked, among other things, about being invited once to dinner at the home of a college classmate whose father happened to be a plantation official. When the conversation turned to the evolution of social trends in the islands, the student, who was familiar with the currency of thoughts on campus, casually mentioned to this host about sporadic discussions about the possible emergence of trade unionism, which, though anathema to the plantation, seemed inevitable to some students, and that it would behoove the plantations to at least think about such an eventuality. In obvious anger, his host berated him for even mentioning the subject and accused the students of "communist" thoughts. The conversation quickly switched to less sensitive matters. Some hard-core issues were toxic and off-limits in management circles. There was room for argument but not enlightened discussion.

Trade unions would emerge in later years, but for the early immigrants, their concerns were tied to bread and butter issues such as the continuing availability of cheap housing, fuel, firewood, etc. Most were content to let sleeping dogs lie.

Hard-core thinking was also reflected in de facto segregation. However, for the immigrants in Spreckelsville, ethnic segregation was fine and not as divisive as the social planners had intended. It proved to be as fragile as modern-day attempts at nation building through military conquest. Instead, it proved to be a boon to immigrant family stability. Centuries-old ethnic values provided a hedge against currents of unfamiliar social distractions. Ethnic pride, often invoked in response to overt discrimination, evoked a determination to survive in a strange land. Eventually, shared values and public education allowed ethnic values to morph into local values as a prelude to full-blown Americanization. And somehow, parents began to realize that their children could never return to their ancestral homes. Their efforts would turn from ancestor worship to ancestral pride in their heritage to abet the growth of their children into dedicated Americans. Naturally, a few hard-core traditionalists may have demurred, but their children disagreed. Moreover, on major issues, local communities had a way of taking care of their own kind. A united front demanded nothing less than unanimity. They knew that they could not become Japanese. The overall parental contribution to the cultivation of identity and culture as hallmarks of individual and community life became a vital part of their legacy to our generation. Claus Spreckels, in providing an abiding sense of time and place, also became a part of that heritage.

Nascent forms of nationalism that surged through both Germany and Japan in the nineteenth century could very well have shaped our destinies in radically different ways had Spreckels chosen to remain in Germany and had our immigrant parents likewise chosen to remain in Japan. Instead, his legacy and our presence—each of which influenced the cultivation of a burgeoning soil-based culture on Maui, interacted in ways that shaped a merging identity between Spreckelsville and its people. The trademark plantation camps that once defined life in Spreckelsville are now gone. They have returned to dust, in apt metaphoric transformation of a place that once thrived on hope and perseverance.

The saving grace for life in Spreckelsville was that even something as basic as the boss-worker relationship took on a humanistic cant that survived the test of inequities and privileges that certain persons in the plantation hierarchy purposely inflicted on immigrant workers. Personal peaks and valleys marked the way to the evolution of place. Claus Spreckels would have understood the inherent dilemmas that marked his own way to immortality on Maui.

The substantive legacies left by Spreckels were highly significant to the shaping of our lives. According to Jacob Adler, who authored the seminal work on Spreckels titled *Claus Spreckels: The Sugar King in Hawaii*, and who demonstrated a superb capacity for archival research and authorship in the publication of his book, the legacy left by the man is indeed notable, both in depth and in scope.[3]

Judged in the context of a pivotal era of the transformation of the landscape of Maui, Adler concludes that the Hamakua ditch, shepherded to completion by Baldwin and Alexander, must be judged the "greater achievement." Strapped as they were for capital, faced with applying seat-of-the-pants solutions to a daunting physical environment laced with unforeseen legal and ethical constraints, none the least of which were superstitions and native taboos, they persevered to the very end, with a trusted cadre of Japanese immigrant artisans. Given the circumstances, it was, by all accounts, a monumental achievement that was destined to be co-opted thereafter by Claus Spreckels.

In a display of inherent opportunism, Spreckels later negotiated a thirty-year lease, at $500 a year, with a provision that included access to water at maximum capacity for sixty years. Spreckels was quick to grasp the predicament of King Kamehameha's lack of capital to fund a major irrigation project. Spreckels, on the other hand, possessed the wherewithal to tap into mainland capital and sources of the engineering expertise that the project would require. The result was the construction of the Spreckelsville ditch.

It began with the dispatch of Herman Schuster, an associate of Spreckels and key figure in the construction of the ditch, on a four-month trip to Pittsburgh (July 9 to November 5, 1878), to procure the necessary materials and equipment. At construction's end, the Hamakua ditch became part of the Spreckelsville ditch.

The Spreckels ditch initially stretched from the slopes of Haleakala to Central Maui. In 1882, Spreckels proceeded to build the Waihee ditch from the other end of the island, by tapping the streams of the West Maui mountains. For the first time, water flowed into Central Maui from both ends of Maui.

The Hamakua ditch was seventeen miles long and was built at a cost of $80,000. The Spreckels ditch was thirty miles long and was built at a cost of $500,000. The economic impact was enormous. Yet, what escaped the awareness of most of us were the vast social and cultural changes that would be unleashed by the completion of the irrigation systems. The waterborne economic transmission belt that dramatically transformed the physical landscape of the island also unleashed changes that altered the social fabric of Maui. A "hydraulic culture" like that of China evolved on Maui, by turning an island of sleepy isolated village enclaves into a vibrant island community energized by industrialized sugar production. The arrival of immigrant laborers from around the world laid the foundation for the growth of a polyglot society. Far from creating ethnic divisiveness, they bonded in shared adversity and healthy appreciation of their differences. Most importantly, they found something significant of themselves in the process, which enabled them to move forward toward integration into a local "Hawaiian" culture. It made Hawaii a unique place to become American.

Spreckels continued in search of natural springs and wells to enhance the development between Kahului and Spreckelsville. By building an electrical plant in Iao Valley, he sought to generate enough electricity to run a string of pumping stations to boost the availability of water. He demonstrated the feasibility of large-scale irrigation to create the largest sugar plantation in the Hawaiian Islands. The government revenue that he generated enabled the Hawaiian Kingdom to prosper handsomely. It also inspired confidence in Hawaii as a market for business investment.

In 1880, he contracted with the San Francisco Iron Works to construct a sugar mill on Maui. Thereafter, three additional mills were built on the island. At the Kahului Port, which was one of only two ports of landing in Hawaii, he maintained his own landings and warehouses, thus making him a favored customer of the Kahului Railroad Company. He established a central telephone system that linked Paia, Spreckelsville, and Wailuku to other plantations. He built large store in Kahului with a branch in Sprecekelsville, which we referred to as Camp One Store. The stores sold everything, from tools, fishing gear, clothing, and watches, to food and staples. By 1884, the main store gained the distinction of being "one of the largest and best appointed stores in the islands," with a volume of business of about $50,000 a month. By 1892, the plantation was regarded as the "largest sugar estate in the world."

Technological enhancements improved production during Spreckels's time. The appearance of a five-roller mill that markedly increased juice extraction from sugarcane was well ahead of the times.

The method of burning green trash and by-products economized on the use of coal in getting the mills up to steam at a time when other mills were using bagasse, a by-product of crushed cane stalks that had to be dried first.

The Spreckelsville mill was the first in the islands to be lighted by electricity, preceding the electrical lighting of Iolani Palace by five years. In that regard, Maui was way ahead of many US mainland communities.

Spreckels was the first to employ railroad transportation, in 1881, for the large-scale hauling of sugarcane, thereby supplanting the use of mules and oxen for hauling to the Port of Kahului. Access to fields where there were no permanent tracks was abetted by an ingenious application of portable tracks carried on the shoulders of short, wiry men of legendary strength. For good reason, they were referred to as "iron men."

The introduction of a controlled irrigation system allowed labor costs to be reduced by enabling one man to irrigate thirty acres a day. The previous method allowed one man to irrigate two acres a day. The employment of mules and oxen was further supplanted with the introduction in 1880 of steam plows. Sprecekels was the first to do so. He was also first to employ fertilizer and cost analysis to the plantation.

His success as a capitalist in transforming the economy of Maui ended, ultimately, with failure in financial capitalization. The Depression of 1884, followed by another depression in 1892 produced crippling financial setbacks for Spreckels. In the family turmoil that followed, Claus and sons John and Adolph were ousted from the Hawaiian Commercial and Sugar Company (HC&S), allowing sons Gus and Rudolph to wrest control of the company. Gus and Rudolph were soon confronted by challenges to their control by a Hawaiian syndicate.

Alexander and Baldwin ultimately became the agent in Honolulu for the company. In 1926, the California-based HC&S company was dissolved and was incorporated in Hawaii under the leadership of H. P. Baldwin and F. F. Baldwin, thereby ending the saga of the "sugar king of Hawaii."

In summation of the complex personality of a man who would be "king," there is an artfully succinct and insightful description of Spreckels provided by A. Grove Day in the foreword to the seminal and much-valued work by Jacob Adler, to whom so much of the archival information contained in this chapter is owed. (The book is titled *Claus Spreckels: The Sugar King in Hawaii*.) It reads,

A fearsome invader of the Hawaiian Islands during the years 1876 to 1903 was Claus Spreckels (1826-1908) who dominated the economic scene with bold designs and cunning corruptions.[4]

It was an apt summation of the legacy of Claus Spreckels in Hawaii and, in particular, in Spreckelsville, Maui.

CHAPTER 3

Bridging the Oceanic and Cultural Divide

Ask counsel of both times of the ancient time what is best, and of the
latter time what is fittest.

—Sir Francis Bacon, *Of Great Place*, 1905

The first contingent of Japanese immigrants to Hawaii departed from
the Port of Yokohama on May 17, 1868. The ship of conveyance was the
Scioto, and amid the documents tucked into the drawer of the ship's purser
was a passenger manifest carrying the names of 142 men and 6 women from
Japan. That they were embarking on a journey of unknown consequence to
Japan's long-term future was arguably the least of their individual concerns.
They were bit players in a drama of historical evolution yet to be played
out to its fullest. Even as individuals, their lowly deportment symbolized
a larger and even more pressing national quest for modernization that
Japan faced as the twentieth century loomed ominously. The country was
now confronted by the proverbial challenge of the West. Japan itself was
treading in troubled waters as the immigrants set sail for the Sandwich
Islands, a name aptly coined upon their discovery by British Captain James
Cook on January 19, 1778. Just as Cook marked the arrival of the West
in Hawaii, the islands were now destined for a Japanese presence on their
shores. While Horace Greeley exhorted young Americans to "go west," the
Japanese were similarly encouraging their people to go west—with the east
wind at their backs.

With the downfall of the Tokugawa Regime, Japan found itself at a
critical historical juncture. A restive new Meiji oligarchy looked on in utter
dismay at what a policy of feudal political control and insularity had done
to the nation. Like so many other countries of the Far East, Japan had fallen
behind the West. Buoyed by the progressive currents of the Renaissance,
philosophic and scientific thought thrived in ways that propelled Europe

into an era of the Industrial Revolution and, ultimately, an expansive surge in nineteenth-century European nationalism. When American Commodore Perry sailed his ships into Japanese waters, it became obvious that Japanese cannonball gunnery was no match for the explosive firepower of Perry's ships. Moreover, Japan's sailing vessels were hardly a match for the steam-powered ships of Perry's fleet. Japan was forced to answer the knock on the door by strangers at its doorsteps.

The dreaded arrival of the West stirred the Japanese to nationalistic fervor. The new Meiji leadership adroitly rallied the nation around the emperor as the preeminent national symbol of state. It produced a national identity in a way that a feudal oligarchy was not able to achieve in over 250 years of military-induced rule. The basic building block for change during the Meiji era began with the institution of a Prussian-inspired constitution that in effect turned Japan into a modern parliamentary government serving under the aegis of the emperor. Moreover, the transformation of rule was cleverly orchestrated as a "gift" of a benevolent emperor to the people of Japan rather than a system foisted on the nation by radical revolutionaries. It thereby provided the new leadership a respite from domestic instability, which allowed the new leadership to buy the precious time that it needed to jump-start the transformation of the nation. Domestic discontent was avoided by pointing to what was occurring abroad, particularly in China. They pointed to the opium trade in particular and asked rhetorically whether the Japanese themselves would like to be turned into a nation of addicts and foreign domination. A classic reliance on foreign threats to sovereignty galvanized a nascent national will to oppose foreign intervention in Japan. Radicals posed their own threat to political stability with a rallying cry to "Revere the Emperor and expel the foreigners." But stability was abetted by the presence of cooler heads.

Included in the drive for modernization and national empowerment was the socially dominant peasant class, long regarded as the harbinger of the nation's rice culture and conservative Japanese cultural and traditional thought, from which later Japanese immigrants would be drawn. When they left for places such as Hawaii, they were not a nationally disaffected group. Many instinctively realized that the nation was in a beleaguered state and that they had somehow become part of the national solution. Most left with the intention of returning to Japan, which aided their state of mind as they left their homeland. Most of the first pioneering group would return, but they established an important precedent for future immigration initiatives. The makeup of future immigrant groups to be sent abroad would be different. But embedded in the subconscious of the people pioneering the first attempt was that they were part of a new Meiji zeitgeist that the nation needed to hastily transform itself.

Upon arrival in Honolulu, the bridging of a yawning cultural divide was one of many issues confounding the initiation of the first group of immigrants into island life. After seemingly interminable days of seaborne travel spent in what one can imagine as grossly unpleasant steerage holds, they were relieved to be on land again. But like all soulful adventurers, they were left to ponder the certainty of an uncertain fate that awaited them beyond the gangplank landing that placed them in Honolulu. Initially, genuinely effusive greetings of *aloha* from native Hawaiians lifted their spirits. But it did little to assuage their innermost doubts and fears as *gaijin*, or foreigners, as the term is used even to this day by the Japanese themselves to refer to "outsiders" venturing into Japan either as tourists or guest workers. They were part of a phenomenon that attested to Japan's own insularity. The *zoris*, or "flip-flops" that they brought along with them to Hawaii ruefully captured the irony of the slipper now flip-flopping over to their own stewardship in Hawaii. They were presenting themselves as *gaijin* on foreign shores. They were bit players, not stalwarts in the drama of modernization being enacted on a worldly stage. But the implications of their journey were enormous. They were part of a desperate Japanese move to keep the nation intact while keeping predatory threats of Western encroachment at bay. Economic depression and demographic pressures were issues that had to be addressed immediately for the sake of national survival. And so, on that footnote began their initial encounter with Hawaii.

Docking at the port of Honolulu, soon enough, the cold formality of dockside procedures returned them to wary contemplation of their unknown fate. The lack of precedence to guide dockside procedures was compounded by the fact that although they exited Japan with tacit governmental approval, they arrived in Hawaii without officially sanctioned documents from the Japanese government. The fledgling Meiji government, still mired in more pressing matters of domestic political consolidation, was not yet geared to tend to the full range of documentation governing international diplomacy. The sense of isolation that the first immigrants experienced mirrored the quandary of Japan struggling to emerge from over 250 years of self-imposed isolationism. Up until then, the only window to the West had been provided at Deshima, a tiny man-made island connected to the Port of Nagasaki by a narrow causeway, where a handful of Dutch traders from the Dutch East Indies Company were allowed to ply their trade in foreign commerce. Deshima was a de facto prison. The Japanese themselves were intolerant of different-looking "foreigners." Years later, during World War II, many of those immigrants would suffer a similar fate by being dragooned into concentration camps just because they looked like enemies. Through the tiny window that the enclave at Deshima offered, Japan maintained a rare and invaluable glimpse into the ways of the West. But the window was hardly wide enough to provide them with something as basic as mundane procedural documents that they needed to enter another country.

The immigrants were part of a pioneering venture, and, like pioneers everywhere, there was scant assurance of ironclad government support for their unprecedented entry into foreign waters. It was sink or swim in waters already roiled by tides of change being wrought by Western galleons plying the Pacific waters with virtual impunity.

The hegemony of the Hawaiian Kingdom was also under siege, mirroring, in like fashion, the similarly arresting concerns of the Mikado over a foreign presence in Edo Bay.

On arrival in Honolulu, host Hawaiian government officials standing astride the *Scioto*, expected the arrival of a contingent of laborers and coolies to work the sugarcane fields of Hawaii. What they got instead were mostly nonlaborers. To be sure, a sprinkling of farmers and ordinary workers were among them, but the dominant group consisted of displaced samurai, artisans, cooks, etc.—men who, by temperament, were not suited to menial labor, let alone the highly impersonal and brutally harsh ways of *lunas* (field bosses) that they would eventually encounter in the sugarcane fields of Hawaii. And field bosses, many of Southern European origin, who were not particularly enamored of strangely unfamiliar Asians or Asian ways and unwilling to let go of an opportunity to lord it over a new crop of beleaguered strangers with no status or constituency in the islands, found a likely target upon which to unleash their stunted need for increased island social status.

The newly arriving Japanese, accustomed to a rigid form of hierarchical relationship that pervaded the ancient feudal system in Japan, probably hoped that personal loyalty would be a fundamental tenet of recognized authority in Hawaii as well. They were more familiar with a form of loyalty cultivated in a humanitarian culture of mutual personal obligations. Although summary enforcement of disobedience in ritual and practice that they had learned to observe in feudal Japan could be brutal and unrelenting, it was administered for tacit moral cause, not for gratuitous and sadistic cause. It was like the guiding principle of army draftee life— to wit, "yours is not to question why; yours is but to do or die." In the military, we saluted the rank of an officer and not necessarily the person. Under Japanese serfdom, it seemed like the character of the man behind the rank counted for more. Whatever the plight of serfs everywhere, the concept of personal loyalty was integral to the success (or failure) of indentured servitude. That's the way the immigrants saw it. Old ways died hard, and the sheer coercion that marked the forging of a coldly impersonal contractual system for which the plantation labor system was noted, quickly became part of the immigrant awareness. Right or wrong, it made many of the neophyte Japanese immigrants feel as if they were being deprived of their humanity. Whippings, however brutal, administered in loyal subservience to a just and shared cause was endurable in feudal Japan. But physical or psychological coercion devoid of a governing principle of loyalty to shared causes was not, even in the world of Tokugawa serfdom. Moreover, most of the first contingent was not ordinary peasants. They were educated people.

The cumulative result of the first attempt at immigration: right idea, faulty assumptions on both sides of the oceanic and cultural divide. Some of the Japanese adventurers stayed in the islands even under those conditions. Most returned home to Japan. The first Japanese attempt at immigration fizzled. But important lessons were learned.

It took another seventeen years to restore reality to Japan's immigration policy. By then, the governing parameters for change had also been drastically altered. This time, the immigration agreements that ensued led to migrations to places as far flung as Canada and Latin America, as well as the United States. By then, the urgency to enact stopgap immigration legislation was apparently being regarded as being even more compelling in Tokyo. Japan was in serious economic straits, and as pressures for domestic economic relief threatened the stability of the new political leadership, the necessity for bold measures intensified.

Meanwhile, among a myriad of events, fate intervened with the arrival of a Hawaiian goodwill mission to Japan, led by King Kalakaua himself. The emergence of nascent nationalism in Japan coincided with a similarly rising sense of nationalism in Hawaii. Hawaiians and Japanese alike faced the threat of Western domination of their countries. The "Merry Monarch," favorably disposed to what he saw and experienced in Japan, provided personal impetus to the idea of an immigration agreement between labor-short Hawaii and labor-abundant Japan. King Kalakaua reportedly even went so far as to propose an alliance sealed in marriage between Princess Kaiulani of Hawaii and Prince Fushimi of Japan. The Japanese emperor demurred on the marriage proposal but supported the immigration proposal. To Japanese officialdom, the personal commitment of the Hawaiian monarch to the pending agreement was sufficiently reassuring to move ahead with a second attempt at immigration.

It also led to the introduction of a key facet of Japanese immigration policy. Even in isolation, the Japanese government leadership had been acutely mindful of the pitfalls that had beset the path-breaking Chinese immigrant experience in America. Gross cartoon caricatures depicting the Chinese, spread by the US media and exacerbated by word-of-mouth rumors about the threat of a "yellow peril" in America, alarmed the Meiji leaders, who were intent on making a favorable entry into the new world of diplomacy. To forestall such a threat to their own migrants, they initiated rigid screening processes to weed out potential "undesirables" from the second contingent of immigrants going abroad. Idealistically, they wanted even the lowliest of the immigrant ranks to become Japanese "ambassadors" to foreign countries. In the short term, their assumption proved naive. To ordinary Americans, the Japanese were no different from the Chinese. "Seen one oriental, you've seen them all," was the operative attitude, and within that initial frame of mind, the Japanese were not seen as deserving of any better treatment than their Chinese counterparts in frontier America. And after all, Native American Indians had fared even worse. As implausible as the attempt at low-level diplomacy may have seemed at first, in our own minds, the long-term result was significant. The ripple effect of that original policy of restraint and orderly conduct inculcated among that early group of Japanese immigrants resonated down to places as remote as Spreckelsville, Maui, where self-imposed social order and respectful behavior as "Japanese" became the norm for local plantation camp life. People saw to it to take care of potential aberrant behavior among "their own kind" out of a remote but compelling sense of duty to what began as governmental prompting. No shameful behavior to the Japanese community was tolerated. The gratitude that we feel today toward the first generation of immigrants who guided us toward meaningful progression in American life was again reflected in the saying, *okage same de*, meaning, "We are what we are because of you." It is a legacy of respect that thrives and survives to this very day as a key element of our own identity as Americans.

The first generation endured rank discrimination. In varying degrees, so have most immigrant groups around the world. But it was obviously more advantageous to be of European rather than Asian stock. And individual acceptance was far easier than "herd" acceptance. But in Hawaii, it was not all about blatant racism. To be sure, racism was a factor; perhaps a dominant factor at the outset of immigrant relations in the islands. But in time it became only one of a mélange of contending factors that would define our island identity. Some cynics referred to it as "mongrelization." Our immigrant parents would probably have understood, since they had arrived in the islands with their own biases and discriminatory views about other races and cultures. But immigrant life had a way of curbing their own cynicism with healthy doses of reality—none the least of which was the realization that fate discriminates. Some are lucky; some are not so lucky. It was somewhat akin to the Orwellian view that all men are created equal, but some are more equal than others. Fate was starkly evident, particularly for Asians. The Japanese said, *shikata ga nai*. The Chinese said, *mei fadze*. Koreans said, *amugotto halsu opsumnida*. In pidgin English, which we shared, it was, "No can help eh!" All of that was integral to a lexicon of fate that we could share with equanimity at the lowest rungs of the social ladder. That was precious, even though it was an unconscious part of our childhood upbringing. Life was not about equality. It was about making equal opportunity a self-help project for living. Objectivity began curbing overriding subjectivity with something as elemental as growing up with an infectious regard for things and friends around us, even if they were "different." The so-called "melting pot" in Hawaii would never have evolved otherwise. To recognize racism as part of our own makeup was to learn to recognize the deep-seated racism that exists and will continue to exist all over the world. Theorists of all stripes may belabor the emergence of liberty in America in arcane terms, but for the unknowing and untutored among us, it was about "feeling good" about fundamental choices without highly reasoned prompting. All of that made our eventual entry into the world of academic learning that much more meaningful later on in life.

Thus, in bridging the cultural divide that greeted them in Hawaii, the most important result of the early Japanese immigrant experience may have come from an intuitive grasp of our own personal shortcomings relative to the goal of achieving self-realization for success in America. Humility counted, and, luckily, Japanese culture and society had a way of pounding that into the minds of their citizens. Not knowing how to say it in Japanese, we referred to the methodology as "kick-in-the-ass" discipline.

Being Asian in America at the turn of the nineteenth century meant second-class citizenship, working in jobs well below individual educational and substantive skill levels and restricted access to opportunities that our children now take for granted. In one of my first encounters with a West Coast-bred Japanese American graduate student at the University of Michigan, I was astonished to learn that in his first meeting as an undergraduate with a college counselor at a West Coast university, he was asked what he would like to enroll in. Unsure of himself as an incoming freshman, he replied, "I don't know for sure, but maybe I can try teaching," to which his adviser immediately and matter-of-factly snapped, "Forget it; nobody will hire you," in this state. I was vaguely aware of such attitudes in Hawaii, but I had never experienced it firsthand. Being from insular Hawaii, that was inconceivable to me, and it literally knocked me back on my heels.

Life, as defined for us as immigrant children on Maui, had to begin with an understanding of ourselves as well as the array of challenges that confronted us. That again was a parental dictum. The ultimate source of our understanding of life had mythological as well as realistic roots. In my mind, none more so than the lessons contained in the classical quote from the eminent Chinese sage Sun Tzu, who warned, centuries ago, that misguided personal thoughts could very well be the source of one's own undoing. It was a code adopted by the Japanese Samurai, whom we were taught to revere as exemplars of moral and ethical conduct. It reads,

If you know your opponent, and you know yourself,

you will always win.

If you don't know your opponent, and you know

only yourself, you will win only part of the time.

If you know neither your opponent nor yourself,

you will always lose.[5]

In the immigrant era, when barriers to progress appeared to be insurmountable, hope had a way of cautioning prudence. To be prudent was to be realistic. The immediate step toward winning was reduced to not losing. Like good bamboo scaffolding, the guiding principle was, bend but don't break. To be realistic was to avoid succumbing to self-defeat. Success or failure may ultimately be determined by fate, but adherence to discipline and moral principle was needed to sustain hope. Ordinary people became "groupies," with individual responsibilities to uphold shared hopes. Falling short of that ideal, there was no one to blame but oneself. To do otherwise was to degrade the cohesiveness of family and community. As children, we balked at the day-to-day behavioral standards imposed on us, but that was the way we learned individual responsibility. *Gyogi*, or proper decorum, was the starting point of accepting moral authority. Parental influence was transmitted through quiet sacrifice that they demonstrated at every level of family responsibility, be it a full day of back-breaking toil or tending to the unending needs of their children. Children instinctively sensed and appreciated the level of sacrifice that was being made by parents for the sake of the family. Children could do little to lessen the stresses and strains being endured by parents, but the fact that the children cared made a world of difference to parents intent on keeping families together. Family ties were thereby forged in soul, and human attributes gained thereby contributed to the stability of the community in Spreckelsville. Families that suffered, ate, spoke, and laughed together and, in spite of minor childhood conflicts, stayed together. Unselfish individual contributions to family stability became integral parts of the genealogy of family life in Spreckelsville. There were misfits, of course. That was an accepted part of ordinary people with no claim to exceptional human traits. But strong families allowed them to take care of their own kind. That was duty. But it also laid a responsible foundation for the principle of individual liberty that following generations of immigrant children would adopt as disciplined Americans. Sun Tze's statement of principle was not immediately compelling or part of our collective awareness as children, but over the years, it became embedded in our subconscious as a valued strategy for civic growth and maturity.

One of the amazing aspects of early plantation life was the way in which ancient allegorical principles survived to guide us in our lives amid the mindless and repetitive tasks of plantation life. Little did we know that the grudging performance of such mind-numbing tasks would someday translate into an understanding of the importance of a culture of meaningful commitment. The tasks at hand may have appeared senseless and demeaning to young minds, but the end result was the emergence of a work ethic that ensured progress. A commitment to excellence in the performance of even the most menial tasks led to an empathetic grasp of what the Japanese called "on," which we understood to mean an enduring moral commitment to responsibilities that radiate from families to friends and community. We lived in a web of culture that reduced timeless principles to simple lessons about secular faith. Human resilience and dogged determination, all endured without complaint, became hallmarks of the chosen way to survival and renewal. We could see and, most importantly, "feel" the stress endured for our sake by committed parents who gave more than they received, although it did not seem that way when they demanded that we do the same as part of our own self-discipline. Beyond family circles, it allowed people who were not particularly fond of each other to work toward a common good. That was the price of liberty to be sought in humble faith. It taught us to become "us" as part of an enduring faith in the possibilities of unselfish cooperative effort. It bred pride in our shared identity even under the straitened circumstances of plantation life. It created bonds that cut across ethnic lines, thereby diminishing the corrosion of envy that could have dominated gratuitous feelings against those who were more economically privileged than we were. The lore and myths of ancient tradition became an integral part of our own historical evolution, even in revisionist form. Beyond the bane of plantation exploitation, we began to understand the promises of capitalism and, in particular, of Keynesian economics. In the minds of simple folks seeking some form of redemption, there was room for at least some form of enlightened government policy, whatever it may turn out to be. Like the sugarcane slips that they patiently placed with furrowed precision into the soil of Maui's cane fields to sustain continued plant growth, the first generation of Japanese immigrants in Spreckelsville devotedly planted the seeds of sustenance and growth for our own young lives. It all began with a fundamental understanding of what our parents and families, rich or poor, meant to us.

As children, we balked, but parents and families set day-to-day behavioral standards to inculcate values that transcended our wayward self-interests. The mode of influence was quiet sacrifice—of demonstrated behavioral values over empty rhetoric.

Immigrant parents appeared to know little, if anything, about capital investment. But to impressionable kids, their grasp of investment in human capital, given the times, was faultless. The social capital that resulted from their investment in our upbringing produced a sense of community that was invaluable to the civic health of Spreckelsville and, ultimately, to our devotion to Hawaii and to America. The cultivation of values began at home, not in classrooms. Not all kids were expected to turn into scholars. But all were expected to be good kids. Some kids failed, but on the whole, the homespun lessons gave us a sense of shared family responsibilities and an identity that abetted our entry into American public education. It prepared us for the multicultural and ethnic integration that was evolving naturally and without social rancor in Spreckelsville with plantation camp names as diverse as Spanish Camp, Russian camp, and Cod Fish (Portuguese) Row. Home and parentage were where it all started and where rigid discipline and harsh standards of personal conduct ruled until our liberation into adulthood, at which point, the cutting of apron strings was decisive. It gave us a better understanding of the price of liberty in a democratic society. Education was an amalgam of hard knocks and liberating thoughts that we were not allowed to take for granted as children. To rebel against such standards was to merit a swift slap on the head by teachers acting on behalf of parents. Parents never apologized for spankings, and we never expected them to. Properly conceived, a resounding kick in the butt promoted stability in our pilgrimage to progress.

Discrimination has always been the expected lot of immigrants the world over. But in Spreckelsville, a culture of faith in fortitude and endurance, firmly embedded in identity, enabled immigrants not only to survive but to establish a firm foundation for shared local values. It was a bonding mechanism. The abiding mantra of early Japanese immigrant life was, again, understanding oneself as a way to an understanding of others. And somehow, it helped us to establish our own bona fides in communities such as Spreckelsville. Humility steeped in inner strength and self-realization demanded of us by parents guided us to tolerate other fellow immigrants. The past would allow us to move forward not as Japanese but as locals in a plantation culture. A mutual grasp of self-help worked. In a world of simple virtues, we never worried about placing our homes, cars, or other private possessions under lock and key. It was a blessing to live in safety and inner contentment, even in the hardest of times. For the have-nots, wealth meant something more than money in the bank.

In hindsight, here again, parents seemed to have been guided in their own convictions by the tradition and culture of Old Japan. The conversion of fiefdoms to private property was achieved at considerable cost and sacrifice to farmers during the early Meiji era. The rice culture was historically carried on the backs of a valued and resilient peasant class, and they now faced a new challenge, crucial to the fortunes of a New Japan. Their conservatism was deeply rooted in convention. Life followed the inherent life cycle of rice cultivation. They were wedded to nature and a lifestyle framed by irrigated paddies and the precise, back-breaking toil that demanded a complete devotion to details. Ironically, during the turbulence of the Meiji Reformation, instead of succumbing to the heady revolutionary disorder of change, which would free them of the rigid constraints of the rice paddies, they became agents of stability. Just as they endured the foibles of nature that governed success or failure in their harvest of crops, upon arrival on Maui, they went with the flow of island tides. Their stoic acceptance of new economic realities abetted a shift from feudal partisanship to the stability of national political bipartisanship. Rightfully, they were revered under the feudal system as a valued social class for their productive contributions to Japanese society. For centuries, they were the pillars of economic and social stability, and stability was a key to the modern transformation of Japan. Japan's conversion to modernity was stunning, only because it was a national effort grounded in the reality of changing times. The taxing blows delivered on both the financial and human capital resources of the nation resonated among farmers. Exorbitant land taxes and inordinate debt burdens, compounded by unstable market prices for rice and the perennial threat of poor harvests, compelled the peasantry to consider immigration as an alternative to an unpredictable future of Japan. Government bailouts and the benevolence of caring feudal lords were by then out of the question. Immigration presented one way out of national quandary. Choice hinged on necessity. *Shikata ga nai!* What else could they or the government do? And so began the saga of Japanese immigration abroad. It would become a source of our legacy, even in far-off Spreckelsville.

The Japanese immigrants came to Hawaii as sojourners, not settlers. A thin reed of hope for a rich and triumphal return to Japan was a powerful goad to survival and accommodation in Hawaii. Eventually, harsh realities, both in Japan and the United States, would disabuse them of any thoughts of a return home to Japan. Fate decreed otherwise, and they became US immigrants. Dreams lapsed into hope and *gaman*, or perseverance, took on added meaning for survival. Some found religious solace in prayers to *kami-sama*, a generic term for god in general. Insecurity had a way of doing that. But for most of the new immigrants, the larger concern was "being Japanese," which translated into fearing failure, rather than pain. It was all about "saving face," the price of being Japanese under hardened circumstances. The strong adhered to that belief. The weak played the blame game. Nervous laughter became the first line of defense against "fresh off the boat" missteps. Their equally nervous peers understood that very well. Stepping off the gangplanks of ships that transported them to Hawaii, they still found themselves "still in the same boat." Notions of "equality" fell by the wayside. Shared circumstances necessitated a forging of personal links that ranged beyond the tawdry constraints of pedigree that prevailed in the old country. They had taken the first step into a democratically inspired social order without even realizing it. Shared values made them into an immigrant group better prepared to adapt to American ways even in the face of racial barriers. "Them" was ultimately transformed into "us," something they could grasp from the Japanese experience of treating the in-group as "us," and the out-group as "them."

Moreover, little did they know that they had arrived at a critical historical tipping point. Like the enlightened Meiji leadership, in an environment of pronounced estrangement from Western-inspired requirements for modernization, a fundamental need to survive and thrive in the new world forced them to come to terms with who they were and what they stood for. In the process of self-realization, they instinctively grasped the importance of bonding with fellow countrymen of differing class, prefectural, and regional biases, who spoke Japanese with differing dialects. They may have not liked or respected each other when they first arrived on Maui, but a common good somehow emerged as a pressing need for all of them. It was an enlightened act of accommodation that would eventually spread to relationships with other ethnic groups that made Spreckelsville what it was for our generation. For us, there was no theoretical explanation. It just happened that way. For locals, it was, "Who cares?" It made us even more local.

Ethnic integration was abetted by a fitful start toward intermarriage. There were old-world animosities, economic and social needs to "stick together," and pronounced cultural differences to contend with. The omnipresence of a cultural divide was further accentuated by the organization of the plantation system into ethnic enclaves. It would take the emergence of a local culture to break down the overarching segregation that divided the locals.

Meanwhile, on a wider plane, intermarriage between the few single Japanese workers from the earliest contingent who had opted to stay in Hawaii and Hawaiian women, prior to the arrival of Japanese "picture brides" in Hawaii, was one consequence of an earlier relationship between Japan and the Kingdom of Hawaii. Japanese men, who found themselves as foreigners, perched on the stoops of welcoming Hawaiian homes, looked in on Hawaiian life, liked what they saw, and became part of Hawaiian homes. Race and ethnicity played minor roles in that integration process. It occurred quite naturally, setting a significant precedent to make Hawaii what it became for us as second-generation locals.

For the first generation of Japanese immigrants in Spreckelsville, first and foremost, life in a strange new environment required that they bond together, for practical reasons, as "Japanese." Being "Japanese" was to be a key to their survival in a strange land as a group of individuals who had grown up identifying their places in society along rigid social class lines. Hence, there was a need, at the outset, for the immigrant flock to organize themselves in accordance with familiar cultural norms, just to survive. Japanese immigration policy saw to it that there were potential "leaders" to guide the early immigrants in the process. They made sure that literacy was a primary requirement to ease the Japanese into immigrant status.

With the outbreak of war against Japan, many of those immigrant "leaders" were jailed as suspected Japanese spies. In the minds of those well-meaning immigrant men, they had come to Hawaii to do "good," and, if possible, even to do "well" financially, but instead, many of them ended up in jail for the duration of World War II. The charge: they had Japanese names, and they were literate! Their presence, particularly in the plantation camps, had made them indispensable to immigrants unable to handle bilingual written communications, particularly those involving intergovernmental regulations. The indispensable role that they voluntarily performed for the good of the early immigrants made them, instead, suspected agents of espionage. In the orderly society that they tried to cultivate in the plantation camps, they found, instead, the wrath of fate visited on them that all-out war with Japan had provoked. *Shikata ga nai* was again all they could say in fatalistic accommodation. In stoic compliance, they never complained publicly or filed suit for the injustice that they suffered. For the young, there was only Japan to blame for the complex web of events that engulfed their families. In a culture of order that their families endeavored to establish in the plantation camps and where there was little need for police patrols, the irony was that it created ample space in Maui's jails for the publicly silent sequestering of suspects with no appetite for social protest. Besides, for some somnambulant local authorities, it afforded an opportunity to put a few "Buddhaheads" in their place.

The plantation camps were initially segregated by ethnic groups. But, oddly enough, segregation served to positively reaffirm the ethnic status of the people of Camp Three, where I grew up, as de facto "Japanese," thereby establishing Japanese tradition and culture as the source of the moral and cultural values upon which families relied for survival on Maui. Instinctively, we learned to grasp the importance of a culture far removed from Japan itself, of which we knew or cared very little at the outset. Most importantly, it opened our eyes to the varied cultures of immigrants in the polyglot society that was evolving in Spreckelsville. Democratic roots began to sprout without prompting. An understanding of who we were was not articulated in words. It was affirmed in deeds—real life, everyday deeds that guided our behavior toward those around us. Some of the most poignant analyses of identity formation in Japan were provided in the past by outside observers of Japanese culture, to which our immigrant parents also were beholden.

Kurt Singer, a brilliant German-Jewish scholar who lived and taught at the Tokyo Imperial University prior to the outbreak of World War II and who was also forced to leave Japan under pressure from the Japanese Nazi Party, recognized a kind of "social grammar" underlying the fabric of Japanese society that allowed the country to incorporate foreign concepts into a framework of thought while guardedly preserving traditional Japanese values. Some have referred to the phenomenon as "new wine in old bottles." It was "the fundamental pattern" duly recognized by other scholars such as Fosco Mariani and Chie Nakane as fundamental to an understanding of the way in which the Japanese reacted to the challenges posed by the Sinic World, and in particular, the West, that many of its Asian neighbors had already succumbed to.

In his book *Mirror, Sword and Jewel: The Geometry of Japanese Life*, Kurt Singer offered the following observation:

> It is like a language with its basic indigenous structure or grammar which has accumulated a heavy overlay of borrowed vocabulary; while the outlook of Japanese society has suffered drastic changes over the past hundred years, the basic social grammar has hardly been affected. Here is an example of industrialization and the importation of western culture not effecting changes in the basic culture.[6]

Looking back, one can detect a similar accommodation in the initial Japanese immigrant experience in Hawaii. They made do with what they faced and what they had, while adhering to the structure and grammar of Japanese life. Like Voltaire, who marveled at the philosophical symmetry of Confucian thought that governed the structure of Chinese society, Singer saw a deeply humanistic underlying grammar in Japanese life that governed Japanese daily life.

From the standpoint of the Spreckelsville experience, which many of us perceived at the most elemental level of daily life, reading Kurt Singer had a way of striking a very familiar Japanese chord—a chord that we "felt" but that we were unable to comprehend or express on our own. It was beyond articulation for immigrants and children alike. It took an outsider like Singer to express an understanding of a kind of "cult of nature," rooted in "deep recollections of childhood as patterns for upbringing" to give us a way to grasp a distant but vitally fundamental link to our own heritage.

A case in point: in the plantation camps of Spreckelsville, the sight of mothers walking to the store or simply strolling with infants strapped to their backs was quite common. *Oppa* was what was referred to as carrying a child on a mother's back. We viewed that as perfectly natural and practical. Today, young mothers ferry their children around in baby carriages—a very practical and modern practice in the modern world. Singer saw it differently from a Japanese perspective. He saw in the Japanese way of strapping the child on a mother's back an expression of nature "conceived of as a soothing, nourishing, refreshing source of life, immeasurably benevolent," and "a projection of the mother not separated from her children by a painful process of weaning."

> For years, the child is carried on the back of the mother, strapped or carried in a pouch-like fold of her padded over-garment, sharing in a half-drowsy state her warmth and her rhythm, robbed of his limbs but feeling sheltered and close to her maternal body which to him means life, protection, company and goodness.[7]

Singer's perspective as an "outsider" was an invaluable contribution to Western students of Japanese culture. He contributed insights that were rarely understood by anyone other than the BIJs (Westerners born in Japan). While leaders such as Oda Nobunaga and Toyotomi Hideyoshi were well disposed to selective Western ways, Tokugawa Ieyasu saw Western ways, and particularly Western religion, as threats to the stability of Japan. Thereafter for over 250 years, the Dutch trading enclave at Deshima provided one of only few Japanese windows to the West.

The Western presence was restored during the Meiji Restoration. But the very pronounced tendency to keep all "outsiders" looking "into" Japanese society persisted. But Westerners, and in particular their born-in-Japan children, were able to see Japan through a cultural prism that was unavailable to students studying Japan from remote nations. That was something that the children of Japanese immigrant children born abroad also lacked. We were born with Japanese names, and through our immigrant parents we were able to grasp Japanese customs intuitively but not with much intellectual rigor. Japanese culture, expressed in native gestures, subtle mannerisms, tastes, speech, etc., made us "foreigners" in Japanese eyes, which understandably persists to this very day. In fact, scholars and authors such as Professor Edwin Reischauer, Ruth Benedict, and Donald Richie, to name just a few, and innumerable observers of Japan today, such as Pico Iyer, offer penetrating insights into an evolving Japanese culture in ways that we, as descendants, are incapable of doing. To the long line of learned observers from all corners of the world who gave us of their wisdom, we owe an enormous debt of gratitude. Their vast intellectual contribution to the lore of Japan reduced the limitations of our own more visceral grasp of heritage transmitted by parents. Many of us have been enriched by both sources of knowledge to gain a better understanding of ourselves as Americans. From caring parents, we received all that we could have asked for in our upbringing. The rest of our identity has been left to each and every one of us to define as descendants of a rich Japanese tradition.

Claus Spreckels contributed much to the development of a corpus of technological and organizational thought that provided the cutting edge for change in Spreckelsville. And Spreckelsville became the crucible within which our local character was ultimately shaped.

Mixed marriages, *hapa* (mixed-blooded) kids, and mixed cuisine, all emerged from the grind of that crucible. *Kau-kau* (which meant either food or eating) produced a local belief that the best way to people's hearts was through their stomachs. We didn't call it fusion cuisine in those days. After all, the workers who toiled in the cane fields had simple tastes and no time for fashionable ideas. Yet, somehow, in a common sense, down-in-the-dirt way, the people of the plantation labor camps distilled the teachings of tradition and culture into a philosophic approach to adversity that contributed to the making of a vibrant local culture. We owe it to the first generation of mixed immigrants in Spreckelsville. Raising us as kids was not simply a labor of love and necessity. It was about honor and pride in our relationship to each other. I have traveled to many parts of this earth but every time I hear, "Eh, Brah, Howzit?" I know I am in the presence of a local Hawaiian. Each time, I am restored to a precious identity that is indescribably cool—a precious reminder that the distillates of life that began in Hawaii remain intact and embedded in the spirit of *aloha*.

CHAPTER 4

Childhood Memories

It takes a village to raise a child.

—African proverb

Spreckelsville was our "village." It was framed by an agglomeration of noncontiguous plantation camps, each situated within a mile or so of each other in a veritable sea of sugarcane fields. While the Pacific Ocean was a work of nature, our sea was a stepchild of commerce. The imaginary link between the realm of nature and the gods and our province of mere mortals aptly reflected the forces that shaped our immigrant existence. We became islanders, bestrode of the influence of real and surreal forces. As immigrant children, the redeeming quality of "Spam musubi" (low-level sushi made with canned Spam, instead of fresh raw fish) was likely to be as compelling as concerns about our vulnerability of *obake* (ghosts). They may have been low-level childish thoughts. But they were unfettered thoughts free of noxious politically contrived coercion. It stamped us as local. Sophistication, for good or bad (genuine or pseudosophistication), could await another phase of breeding. Fortunately, the accommodation between man and nature fared well in our plantation village environment. Perhaps it had to do with the tempering influence of the tropics. For whatever reason, Spreckelsville provided us with a landed identity that was important to our grounding as ordinary human beings in need of a will to sustain our confrontation with the dynamic of changes that ultimately shaped the lives of a whole generation of Japanese immigrant families and children.

At the epicenter of the loose configuration of camps that made up Spreckelsville was Camp One, an early hub of importance to a railroad network that radiated out of Maui's most important port, Kahului Harbor. The harbor provided Maui with a vital link to a burgeoning world of international commerce that we were incapable of comprehending. At that point in history, Camp One had the most technologically advanced sugar mill in the islands; it had one of Hawaii's most outstanding retail consumer outlets, a post office, a movie theater that screened Hollywood's latest productions, a vast outdoor athletic facility with adjoining tennis courts, and, of course, a posh and very private country club, around which the beach homes of the plantation elite were clustered. Maui's first hospital was established in Spreckelsville in 1885.

Camp One's aura of energized commerce contributed to a pervasive civic identity that radiated out to the adjoining camps of Spreckelsville. It contributed to our "village" identity. Moreover, the fundamental framework of commerce allowed a locally adjunct web of culture to grow along with it. It was to that web of culture that we were instinctively drawn as denizens of a village that was "country" but not necessarily backward.

The forces that governed technological advancement were, of their very nature, impersonal. But social change also shaped and personalized spontaneous community developments. As a private businessman, my father was frequently called on by early camp residents to cope with emergencies. Before the appearances of public social services, our telephone and car provided conduits for camp residents in need of emergency assistance, particularly medical help. As a child, I remember waking up to late-night knocks on our front door by camp residents seeking help. As one of the earliest owners of a car, either my father or one of my brothers became willing providers of ambulatory assistance to camp residents. There were other unforeseen needs to be taken care of. The development of such a spontaneous system of community assistance brought us closer to plantation camp life.

Even as an aged, former resident of Maui, lingering thoughts about growing up in Spreckelsville still elicit an unerring blend of joy in understanding our immigrant roots. It all began in childhood, and it is still all about "returning home." In a world of restrictive conventions and customs, the liberty to soar in individual joy was an abiding gift. It was the ultimate gift of being born American on Maui. To assent, as a local, to simple pleasures is to place the vagaries of fate in perspective. For the fortunate, to look back positively and not in anger was and still is the ultimate gift of meaningful immigrant life. In what is always destined to be a fleeting encounter with "home," it is far more pleasurable to be transported by treasured feelings than by empty thoughts. In the best of circumstances, mind is restored to soul. Personally, and as an American, the bestirring to "liberty" was first rooted in elementary sensations. It now calls into question the seeming contradiction between the oppressive aspects of an oligarchic plantation system and the basic needs of men and women alike to be "free." How did our forebears cope? Perhaps, the answer resides in the banality of plantation life itself. The banality of ordinary people too preoccupied with livelihood to wrestle adequately with moral issues of right or wrong. Grinding accommodation with reality turned many of us into banal people. It even became part of the woodwork that framed our lives. Looking back with grace and without rancor or despair is the gift of ambient life that has sustained our faith in life as it was in Spreckelsville. Maui, as we once knew it, and Spreckelsville in particular, now exists in name only, no longer animated by the forces and conditions that originally shaped our lives. But that's immaterial. The spirit lives on.

Years ago, when I encountered an ad in a Japanese newspaper that visually depicted a young Japanese teenager reveling in the sensation of an ice-cold bottle of Coca Cola clutched to his face, I, along with some American colleagues, debated as to what the caption "I feel Coke!" really conveyed in translation. The full-page advertisement served as a kind of Rorschach test, as we each weighed in, in jocular banter, about the meaning of the message, which was not grammatically correct in English but strikingly evident in intent. Our opinions were as wide-ranging as they were inconclusive. My own take on the ad was that: it is about the exhilaration of "feel," which transcends conventional parameters of just "taste" alone. I was transported back in feeling to the roots of what I learned in Spreckelsville. Whether I was right or wrong in my interpretation was immaterial. What it did was to reinforce my conviction that proper translation provides a valuable venue to an understanding of cross-cultural messages.

The immigrants in Spreckelsville learned English to cope with American life. It was the key to community bonding. Granted, it was mostly pidgin English. It was language with no syntax or grammar, unlikely conjunctions, but full of meaning at the most elemental level of human communication. To connect with family and community in pidgin was to celebrate humanity, not to calibrate social correctness. No translations required, except for outsiders. It was both defense mechanism and shared identity. It dispelled loneliness in crowded places. In slogging through a quagmire of blatant discrimination faced by Asian immigrants who were calculatingly denied rights of citizenship and, in too many cases; due process, they nevertheless endured in forbearance. Hope for a better future was embodied in their slogan "for the sake of the children!" Besides, if the cashier at the market check-out counter could not understand what "shchew meat" meant, their English-speaking children could intercede by explaining, "She means stew meat." It was slow going, but it made for a stronger union of immigrants and their polyglot community. Sounding silly was okay. It was healthy to laugh at oneself—not others. "Eh, no laugh you," was a common rejoinder, a reminder that we were all in the same boat. Shared adversity required shared understanding, and pidgin was the deliverer of messages.

With pidgin as the medium of the message, surmounting social barriers had a bonding effect, especially on the children. To some outside observers, it reeked too much of tribalism. But, luckily, it was not driven solely by race and ethnicity. In sharing hope, people discovered a measure of humanity within themselves. They were not restrained by self-imposed barriers that would have hampered collective efforts to surmount larger social class barriers. We didn't know why, but we became more inclusive rather than exclusive while preserving our varying ethnic roots. Evolution, not rampant and unstructured progressivism, became the rule for advancement in Spreckelsville. And most fortunately, pain and personal deprivation tempered our resolve to move ahead with our lives. Today, in the comfort of our secure and more bountiful lifestyle, we are prone to forget that part of our legacy, which was an incremental legacy that was so vital to the shaping of our identity. It grounded our understanding of our formative lives in Spreckelsville with homespun levity.

Thus on every return to Maui, as the aircraft descends into a landing pattern at Kahului Airport, I am gripped by anticipation—an incoherent jumble of anticipatory emotions that defies reason. A thousand images flit by the window, and just as suddenly, the visual projection ends. The jolt of rubber hitting the tarmac shakes one back into sobriety. Nativist emotions suddenly succumb to procedure as we shuffle, in robotic sequence, out to the passenger terminal.

On such occasions, imagery mimics memory—sometimes poignantly, at other times faintly, as old age reminds us of the toll it takes on what we remember. Among the feast of all-too-brief images that mark our landings on Maui, one facet of the landscape always stands out above all. It is the iconic imagery of the sugarcane fields.

Sugarcane fields, by sheer dint of visual and subliminal imagery, have always dominated the landscape of Maui as we knew it. The plant itself, identified by botanists as a species of grass, was the dominant symbol of Spreckelsville. It carpeted our community landscape with a shade of green that was visually irrepressible. Yet, by being commonplace, it was also taken for granted, especially by those who had to work in the fields to eke out a living. But as species of grass capable of growing to heights as high as thirty feet, we never thought of sugarcane as grass. As kids, sugarcane was simply too gigantic to equate with the likes of grass that covered our lawns and playing fields. But grass was what it was, and it dominated the landscape of Spreckelsville with untrammeled visual effect. It reinforced, with vivid effect, the image of sugar production and the plantation system as preeminent forces in the economic life of Spreckelsville. Like the disparity between sugarcane and ordinary grass, it brought into sharp relief the disparate roles of capital, management, labor, in tapping into the largess of the land. And in very human terms, it laid out the stage for the human drama that was to make the plantation society what it was in its earliest iteration.

We were naturally unaware that the development of Spreckelsville actually gained impetus in the turbulence of the nineteenth century when industrialization energized the development and applications of science and technology in ways that transformed Western civilization and thought. Hawaii was destined to become part of the sweeping changes that ensued. The arrival of industrialized agriculture ultimately led to the creation of the plantation system that ruled life on Maui. It led to the creation of places such as Spreckelsville.

The plantation system on Maui can perhaps be best described as paternalistic. The central theme was essentially, "We provide; you abide." Reflecting the temper of the times, it was racist, calculatingly divisive, and paranoid in its initial experimentation with social engineering. For the Japanese immigrants, it was not unlike the rudimentary legacies of Japanese feudal life, from which they were not too far removed. *Amae*, or the psychological dependency that comes with the security that they found in free, or at nominal cost, housing, fuel, and communal living facilities, though wanting in many ways, aided their initial adjustment to plantation life.

As a plantation community, Spreckelsville was rather unique in social configuration. Situated at the apex of the social ladder were the plantation elite. They lived in isolated splendor along a stretch of beach that was in keeping with the social expectations of the day. Their homes were large and rambling but never ostentatious. Frank Baldwin, during his time as the patriarch of the clan and president of HC&S, was seen on many a day driving himself to work in a black, midsize Buick, a stark contrast to the splashy cars that the island nouveau riche would opt for in later years. Personal modesty and decorum marked their own regard for heritage. With some exceptions, class, not crass, was their byword. They undoubtedly had their share of internal family problems, including inbreeding. No mixing, genetically or socially, with the locals. But then again, upper-class Asians did the same. And just as plantation camp families tended to refrain from something as troubling and tragic as spousal abuse as strictly private matters to be left to the families themselves, talk about upper-class family problems, either real, rumored, or imagined, tended to be treated as private matters. In a tiny island environment, there were likely to be few secrets. So privacy was protected across the board and not always for the best of reasons. Like troublesome weeds in the garden, selfishness required constant tending, lest they got out of hand.

Midlevel management and professional families employed by the sugar and pineapple industries did not cluster into privileged enclaves. Most lived comfortably in towns such as Wailuku and Kahului, close to the seat of government and better public amenities, as well as in choice locations in the beautiful upcountry regions of Maui. Life in up-country estates and the beachfront homes of Spreckelsville adjacent to the Maui Country Club was the ultimate cachet for privileged living. Some of the most insufferable *haoles* were those who pretended to be part of that pedigree.

The plantation camps of Spreckelsville had no names. Like gulags, they were assigned numbers. Even the workers were assigned numbers, called *bango*. To management, it made sense. Asians in particular had strange-sounding names. On payday, it was easier to call out a number instead of a strange-sounding name. Besides, to *haoles*, Asians all looked the same. Seen one, seen them all. Little did they know that the Asians felt the same way about them. They all looked the same too.

The standard plantation home in Spreckelsville had three bedrooms, an all-purpose living-dining room, and an attached kitchen. Redwood was used extensively in construction to deter termites. Hastily assembled wall boards tended to warp, allowing wind, rain, and dust to filter in, necessitating quick and innovative prevention measures. Old newspapers and cardboard came in handy to fill in the cracks. It contributed to a culture of saving scraps of materials not only to meet contingencies but for the extension of a patchwork approach to life. Not enough money to buy expensive bolts of cloth? No problem. Just stitch together patchwork quilts, for example. The women tended to belittle their handiwork, little realizing that many were real works of art.

The hand scrubbing of floors with scrap pieces of cloth had a way of adding luster to even rough-hewn boards. For the Japanese immigrants, that was supposed to express a measure of self-respect for *uchi*, or home, and for life itself.

Finally, there were the public baths and shared outhouses. In some locations, because of the lay of the land, there was stench. Trade winds helped when inconsistent flows of water in the sewage system produced unwelcome odors. But to the credit of camp residents, public facilities such as baths and toilet facilities were kept clean. Unlike the sorry state of latter-day public facilities, a shared culture of order and cleanliness prevailed. Respect for property thrived, in spite of a poverty of private needs. That was a blessing of awareness. According to Japanese tradition, a long and soothing soak in a large communal bath was invariably preceded by a ritual head-to-toe scrubbing of one's body. Dirt and perspiration went down the drain—not into bathtubs. To do otherwise was to commit the ultimate sin in bathhouse etiquette. *Hazukashi*, or "shameful" behavior, either in public or private baths was akin to engagement in sacrilege in the camps. It was in the contrived "purity" of bathwater that workers found solace for their weary bodies at the end of the day. The huge communal bathtubs became a place for utter relaxation and pleasant conversation. Tensions were released, and ultimately the *ofuro*, or bathhouse, and the simple act of bathing came to be associated with a state of mind. Like in Japan, we took baths at the end of the day instead of showering in the morning. Clean sheets demanded clean bodies at night.

One day in Washington, when a colleague and I were discussing the therapeutic benefits of bathing local style, a courtly and scholarly gentleman overheard our conversation and guffawed at the notion of a state of mind being attached to bathing. He said that he took a morning shower daily simply to cleanse his body, not his soul. He listened intently to our explanations. But at the end of the day, I'm sure he took his shower without paying any heed to what we were talking about. But then again, many of us, too, have naturally succumbed to the unthinking, quick shower routine on the mainland.

Sandwiched between Camps One, Two, and Three was a housing enclave reserved for workers who functioned as field bosses and clerical personnel. The residents there were predominantly Portuguese from the Azores. Hence, the evolution of the name "Codfish Row," in which cod apparently represented one of the gustatory pleasures of the Portuguese community. The homes there were a cut above that of the regular plantation homes. They were larger, and many had private baths, in contrast to the communal baths and toilet facilities shared by residents of the regular camps. More than a mere hint of privilege naturally accrued to its residents.

Half a mile up the road was Camp Three, where I grew up in its periphery. The "main drag" that bisected the camp was made up of four private businesses, a mark of small businesses and private enterprise in infancy. There was the Iwanaga Photo Studio, which my family owned, the Kitagawa Service Station, the Sam Sato Store, and the Yoshizawa Barber Shop. By outward indications, all fared well in the understated privacy that set them apart from plantation life. Market conditions were aided by the stability of plantation employment, even through the Great Depression. Most importantly, they symbolized the possibilities of private enterprise and independent living. Though none of the families belonged to the plantation, each integrated into the prevailing plantation social system. That meant muting earnings and material possessions. All of the small businesses were labor-intensive, requiring inordinate effort, 24/7. Like everyone else, vacations were out of the question. But we were at "liberty," which, even in elemental comprehension, meant a great deal.

Mrs. Sato, mother of Sam Sato, and her daughter-in-law, Gladys, were up as early as 2:00 a.m. to knead the dough and perform a myriad of chores to have their fresh-baked pastries ready by the crack of dawn. Their miniature pies, doughnuts, cupcakes, and manju, all handmade, were legendary in goodness. Today, the generational tradition continues, in the person of Lynn Sato Toma and her husband, Charlie. About a mile away in Camp Two, a similar operation was under way at the Itakura Store with like effect. Over fifty years later, Sam Sato manju and Itakura manju, each distinctive and different but equally delicious to us, have become staples featured at our reunions at the California Hotel in Las Vegas.

Technically speaking, none of the business establishments, including my father's studio, belonged to the camp, but we identified with the camp and the people. We became integral parts of an extended camp life. However, unavoidably, some of us were regarded as privileged. Our homes, attached to store fronts, were much larger and were situated on large plots of land. Our home, located at the leading edge of the camp, adjoined a virgin forest with hundred-year-old pine trees that served as windbreakers for the adjoining cane fields. It made me acutely aware as a child that the trust of the children of the camp had to be earned. In the long run, it made those of us who led separate, private lives more objective about many of the realities of plantation life in Spreckelsville.

There were naturally positive and negative sides to plantation life. The bottom line was that it provided jobs to the accompaniment of hope for immigrant families. For most of the vanguard Japanese immigrants, what they sought initially was not the American dream. They intended to accumulate wealth and then return to Japan. They quickly came to the stark realization that plantation life was suited more to survival than to the sustenance of impossible dreams. There would be no return to Japan in wealth and comfort. With the arrival of their American-born children, they became settlers, rather than sojourners. They then turned to defining the terms of civic and social engagement in Spreckelsville.

From the vantage point of Spreckelsville, the fields that carpeted the landscape were visually stunning and yet hauntingly expressive of the human toll that it extracted from the men and women who worked, day in and day out, to sustain them. It bent the bodies of both men and women, but fortunately, it never broke their will. In the evolution of relations between management and labor, both acquiescence and accommodation proceeded along bumpy paths. There were justifiable grievances, but both sides ultimately understood what it meant to "save face," for the sake of mutual economic advantages. It was not easygoing, but it ameliorated excess militancy on both sides of the social divide.

As to be expected in a plantation system, strife and rancor contributed to varying expectations and goals. To the second generation of immigrants, accommodation evolved into a realization that hard work alone was obviously not enough to confront the limitations of power and influence that the plantation system imposed on progress. Opportunity had to be leveraged. And along the way they asked, "So, what's wrong if I want to become rich and successful too?" At that juncture, hope became something more than a pipe dream. The patience and sacrifice of parents began to take on a new perspective in the minds of their children. Progress entailed multifaceted goals. A hybrid culture spawned hybrid expectations, none-the-least of which was an underlying and growing awareness of the need for meaningful political participation and unionization.

As plantation life evolved in Spreckelsville, at the lowest level of the labor pyramid, a vital merging of man and crop needs also emerged. Daily lifestyles and work became integral parts of the lifeblood of the people. Their understanding of the cycle of life of the sugarcane crops began to replicate their understanding of the human life cycle. Planting, cultivating, and harvesting reflected their own cycle of birth, earthly existence, adulthood, and death. The understanding of life in those terms was visceral and intuitive. They didn't need to be poets of the realm to express that. They simply lived under those terms. Their work ethic was the medium of their message. More importantly, at that stage of plantation life, it engendered a fundamental sense of humility with respect for the mysteries and powers of nature. Pride in their work of coaxing productivity from the soil also translated into pride in their identity as products of a soil-based culture. A distinctive philosophical tendency, rooted in soil, went on to aid the immigrants in codifying a bedrock of values and beliefs that still feeds into our Hawaiian identity. The values that we inherited still resonate in the down-to-earth simplicity of a message that counsels a search for meaning in the complexities of modern urban life.

Like the rice culture that shaped the values of our Japanese immigrant parents, our values were cast in the hybrid mold of a sugar culture—a culture destined to make us deeply appreciative of our Japanese heritage but mindful that we are locals and Americans at heart. In the vibrant polyglot society that was collectively forged, the integrating tool was the English language taught in public schools. Our parents spoke Japanese; we spoke English. That's when a pidgin language appeared to facilitate intergenerational communication. It was "no big deal," simply because it was couched in faith. And in that faith was a spiritual component best characterized by the symbol of the cane field. The capturing of that spirit was perhaps best depicted in an incident described by Joseph Campbell and Bill Moyers in their book *The Power of Myth*.

In Japan for an international conference on religion, Campbell overheard another American delegate, a social philosopher from New York say to a Shinto priest, "We've been now to a good many ceremonies and have seen quite a few of your shrines. But I don't get your ideology. I don't get your theology." The Japanese paused as though in deep thought and then slowly shook his head. "I think we don't have ideology," he said. "We don't have theology. We dance."[8]

The Shinto priest, in unerring and unwitting terms, captured the essence of the spirit conveyed by sugarcane fields stirred to hula (Hawaiian dance) on many a windswept day in Spreckelsville. Life was about rhythm, orchestrated in concert, by man and nature.

It is through those sugarcane fields that one wends one's way by driving on Hana Highway to get to Camp Three Spreckelsville, just adjacent to the airport, where I was born and raised.

My father built his home and photo studio on land leased from the plantation. Like so many other children, I never ever bothered to ask him what brought him to Hawaii at an early age. He never labored in the fields. An introvert by nature, he cloaked a fierce streak of independence with incessant work. He never tolerated just "hanging out" or doing nothing among us. Playing was fine, as long as it involved physical activity and the use of our minds. At the end of the day, he would take long walks through the cane fields in thoughtful contemplation. In solitary thought, he enjoyed moments of unencumbered leisure. The only quiet time that he seemed to approve of was reading. Both he and my mother were voracious readers. We never disturbed him when he was reading. My mother did her reading late at night when all the chores were done and everyone else was asleep. That was her only quiet time.

In the spring of 1972, I finally learned something about my father from his cousin, a private practice physician in Tokyo. He and my father were not just cousins. According to the doctor, they were also "best" friends. Over the years, they exchanged personal mementos that they chose not to leave to their own children. Somehow, when the doctor heard of my visit to Tokyo, he asked his daughter Masako to arrange a meeting at his private residence. I demurred at first, not because I did not want to meet him (I really did), but because I was acutely aware of my poor command of the Japanese language and the situational ethics associated with initial introductions. I was afraid of appearing overly boorish. Much to my relief, I needn't have worried. He was a man of commanding and courtly presence who put me completely at ease. It was a fateful and unforgettable encounter for which I will be forever grateful. Masako was there throughout the private meeting to help me with any lapses in communication.

My father was one of three children—two boys and one girl. The first son became a physician, and my father was also scheduled to enter medical school in Tokyo. According to the doctor, he and my father left Kumamoto Prefecture together to enroll as classmates. For some reason or another, they arrived on campus only to discover that only one vacancy was available on the opening day of classes. That vacancy was filled by my father's cousin with the understanding that he would enter the next class. According to his cousin, my father, who stood five feet eleven and was of strapping physique, was immediately drawn to his favorite sport—sumo or Japanese wrestling, which was thriving in Tokyo. His preoccupation with the sport drew a stinging rebuke from an uncle looking after them in Tokyo, who steered him into learning x-ray technology as a prelude to entry into medical school. The details are still murky, but apparently, out of sheer restlessness and a thirst for adventure, he heard of a recruitment program for work in Hawaii. He thought of going to Hawaii and then returning to attend medical school in Tokyo.

Two thoughts crossed my mind during the conversation. First, as long as I can remember, in his visits to Toda Drug Store in Kahului, he bought every new publication of magazines such as *Better Homes and Gardens*, *Sunset Magazine*, *House Beautiful*, etc., for my mother and literary and sumo magazines for himself. He read every available sumo magazine in Hawaii. It took a visit to his cousin for me to realize why. Moreover, his closest friends in the islands were Japanese-educated doctors who were there to look after the medical needs of the Japanese immigrants in the islands. It made me realize why he always wished that one of his sons would go to medical school. None of us did. To his credit, he never forced the issue of a career choice in medicine on any of us. All he asked of us was to use our college education to find self-realization and happiness in life. He was unrelenting in disciplining each of his children, but once we went off to college, he left us to discipline ourselves and our own children.

It also fits into a statement carried in a book by Lan Cao and Himilee Novas (*Everything You Need to Know about Asia-American History*), in which they wrote that

In an effort to safeguard Japan's honor, the Japanese Government strictly supervised the flow of immigrants from Japan until 1894.

Japanese officials viewed its workers abroad as diplomats who had a responsibility to preserve Japan's fine reputation. Thus the Japanese carefully screened out lowly, illiterate workers and other such undesirables who might jeopardize Japan's honor. Only literate, healthy, strong, and relatively well educated Japanese made the grade for emigration. Japanese officials were determined that the fate of Chinese workers whom the United States barred from immigration with The Chinese Exclusion Act of 1882 would not befall Japan's subjects.[9]

My father was never employed as a laborer because he never had a labor contract. Instead, for the short term, he arranged to go to Hawaii as an adopted son of the Iwanaga family. For the first time in my life, I realized why my father's business was named the Iwanaga Photo Studio. I had never bothered to ask why of my parents. As a carefree child, I thought it was perfectly normal to have two identifying names. Each of the children was registered under Kiyosaki. The business name was Iwanaga. After his arrival in Honolulu, he parlayed his skills as an x-ray technician to support himself. Anxious to set out on his own, he then applied his x-ray skills to become an apprentice to one of the foremost photographers in the islands and began by freelancing on his own in Paia Maui. He prospered enough to purchase two beach homes in Paia as rental property and then moved the family to a rental home on Emma Street in Honolulu. He then proceeded to open a studio at the corner of Nuuanu and Beretania streets. Fiercely opposed to the idea of borrowing money, he was nevertheless forced to take out a bank loan to open his studio. He prospered, especially with the frequent arrival of the US Fleet in town. He worked alone, and on many nights, my sister Cherry had to take his dinner to him as he worked late into the night. He quickly paid off his loan. When the pleased bank officers sent him a letter thanking him for his patronage and an accompanying letter which stated that they would be pleased to serve him again, to my sister's horror, he scrawled *kuso* or "shit" on the return correspondence. Good thing his acerbic comment was written in Japanese and not in English. In my books, he was the last of the Confucians. He abhorred borrowing money or any thought of using people, and he would have disdained the modern-day reliance on credit cards. He was a cash-and-carry man; through and through.

The Great Depression of 1929 forced him to return to Maui, where he built a stucco-front studio, processing lab, and adjoining family residence on the outskirts Camp Three, Spreckelsville. I was born there, the last of six children in our family. Thus began my life in Spreckelsville. Childhood there was wonderful. I didn't even know what the Great Depression meant until I read about it in college. Life was tough economically for my parents, but as a know-nothing infant, I was shielded from all of that. It was a time of simple life—simple needs, and, best of all, the plantation did not fold. People had to eat, and even in hard times, sugar was necessary to human sustenance and pleasure. So was the traditional Japanese regard for photos commemorating births, weddings, graduation, etc., which benefited my father's business.

Our home reflected the privacy that my parents always sought in life. The logic of construction, financed this time with extended family assistance, incorporated those ideals. The studio fronted the main highway, and it was set back so that there was ample parking space. The lab was located on stilts above the plantation irrigation ditch that ran under our home, conveniently situated to take away the runoff from the processing lab and photo-washing machines. The sloping land that extended to the back of the property was also on stilts, which allowed cool breezes to circulate under the home. The space created by the stilts also allowed my father to build a woodworking shop under the home. The elevated structure, which leveled out in the back, also provided a backyard and garden that was out of public view. Amid a manicured lawn terraced with tropical plants and miniature bonsai trees, my father built a unique entertainment court, which we referred to as the Lilikoi Court. It consisted of a charcoal barbecue grill, built right into the middle of a massive dining table/platform built of reinforced concrete and lava rock capable of withstanding the heat from the grill and allowing everyone seated at the table to witness the grilling by my mother, or, if the venue of dining allowed, for each one to do his or her own grilling. The grill itself, which could be covered to provide a table for regular outdoor dining when not in use, was custom shaped by an aged machinist, who took a discarded steel plate from an old junkyard tractor and bored holes into it to cleverly handle the flow of excess drippings. It was a one-of-a-kind creation, ingeniously designed by my father, using materials readily available in various island locales. Sand used for the cement was abundant at the beach; lava rocks were strewn all around island hillsides, just for the taking, and the industrial dump sites provided valuable metallic products—all for free. The creative use of materials, even "junk" was especially necessary during World War II, when everything was in short supply or otherwise unavailable for purchase. Among the long list of people entertained at dinner by my parents during and after World War II in that courtyard was major league pitching great Bob Feller and his wife, who were headed on a barnstorming exhibition tour of Japan in 1947. There were no notable dining spots in Wailuku in those days, or apparently even at the Maui Grand Hotel, where the Fellers were staying. It prompted the president of the Hawaiian Baseball League to ask my father whether he could bring them over for dinner, which my father happily agreed to. It was a common occurrence at our home during my childhood.

Living close to nature and appreciating its gifts was life-enhancing for immigrant life. And the virtual greening of the yards surrounding our home was abetted by an embedded sprinkler system and hand-drawn buckets of water using the irrigation ditch that ran through our leased property. It kept our lawns perpetually green. Our lawns were first carpeted with Bermuda grass but later were replaced with centipedegrass, which was so dense that it naturally impeded the spread of weeds. We had front, back, and side lawns that required repetitive mowing after each raking to smooth out uneven stubs that tended to stick out. It was time-consuming work, but the final effect was to give each of the lawns the look of thick carpeting. For me, the downside was that I had to mow the lawn and trim the edges every weekend. At first, I resented having my playtime reduced by all the yard work every Saturday, but eventually I began to take pride in the manicured look of our lawns. My part in taking on those chores became not my own but a family responsibility requiring no other prompting.

Buying into life began at home. At the most fundamental level of life in Spreckelsville, coherence was defined by responsibility and accountability to one's family. When parents suffered, the children suffered along with them. The role of the quiet but dominant parent was played by stoic fathers who, when necessary, said no to any unreasonable demands by children. Yet, it was the seemingly passive mothers who played the most active roles in family life. They raised the children while their husbands worked. They handled all money matters. They played the key role of making the children understand what it meant to suffer deprivation under plantation life. They did it by giving the children what little there was to give—often leaving nothing for themselves. It was their way of teaching sacrifice. They defined feminism with quiet strength—not self-pity. In her memorable book about the heroism of the Japanese American soldiers of the 100th/442nd Combat Team, Thelma Chang pays eloquent tribute to dying soldiers consistently crying out *okasan*, or "mom," as life expired on the battlefield. It was the ultimate tribute to their portrayal of respect for their mothers.

Underlying the father/mother relationship was the principle of yin and yang, the cosmic expression of dual forces at work. Male-female, active-passive, positive-negative, light-dark—simple principles applied with consistency that stabilized relationships within families. Fathers and mothers in tandem made a difference in the lives of the children. Economically poor; culturally enriched, prosperity was measured by unfettered emotional attachments to parental influence. In hindsight, that was priceless because it also radiated out to the community as a whole.

In the plantation camps, what remains etched in memory are scenes such as uncomplaining mothers rising well before dawn to prepare families for the day. Rice has to be cooked to fill the lunch pails for fathers and working mothers, and breakfast and lunch had to be prepared for the children. While everyone ate, mothers dressed for work in the cane fields or for the never-ending chores of motherhood in plantation life. The morning fare was simple—rice with miso soup, pickles, and side dishes sparsely seasoned with meat or fish. Never in their wildest imagination could the people in the camps even contemplate that standard fare such as sashimi (raw fish) and edamame (soybeans) would someday become parts of modern American cuisine. Strength and family cohesion revolved around mothers. It was a male-dominated culture where wives invariably deferred to their husbands. But the indispensable role that mothers played in holding the family together made them stronger in the long run. In the culture of dependency, even husbands had to fall in line for wives to take care of their everyday needs. In typical Japanese fashion, mothers made light of their role. But it was easy to see why their influence became so dominant in family life.

There was also another significant role that the women of the camps played. In the early days of plantation life, working mothers with babies requiring nursing took their infants along to work in the cane fields, breast-feeding them whenever time and circumstances permitted. It was a constant challenge to find places where the babies could be shaded from the scorching sun or protected from rainfall. They looked in on their babies intermittently, aided by the concern of other women who also kept an eye out for them. The bonding that occurred between mothers and children in those fields was intense, and the social bonding that was facilitated between women of varying races and ethnicity, all of whom understood and shared in the adversity of frontier parenting, was immeasurable. It abetted tolerance between those women, and it brought people together as a community in Spreckelsville.

Fortunately, my stay-at-home mother, who bore six children, never had to work in the fields. But she played roles that brought her closer to the women of the community in other ways. As one of the few bilingual women of the first generation, she provided an informal conduit to Western ways to which many of the camp women had no access.

Plantation life turned people into pragmatists. It also blunted the early influence of nativist ideologies. Simple, homeschooled human virtues, defined by earthy realities, allowed the children to enter plantation culture with tolerance for the needs of a polyglot society. Natural processes allowed racial and ethnic divides to loosen. It began with such ordinary practices as sharing homemade school lunches, usually wrapped in old newspapers. They learned to "talk-story" in pidgin and to laugh at the idiosyncratic ways of each of their own ancestral cultures. It also broke down social barriers by creating allegiances to one another—away from old-world prejudices. Again, it turned us into locals.

The local spirit that animated that culture was also nurtured by abiding recreational pleasures. Games such as "touch base," using selectively designated trees as bases, "pee-o-wee," in which a single broom handle sawed into bat and simulated "ball" provided all the equipment needed to play a game that required great hand-eye dexterity and coordination. We made play swords fashioned out of koa branches and panax hedge plants that peeled easily to mimic blades and scabbards. We made slingshots fashioned from pine tree branches, discarded rubber tubes, and "Bull Durham" tobacco pouches that served as cradles to grip the stones for launching as missiles. In the virgin forest that extended well beyond our home, I spent countless solitary hours with a Daisy Carbine air rifle, plinking every imaginable target. I learned a great deal about nature in that forest. For example, doves and mynah birds always perched themselves at the top of the highest trees, which made them impervious to shots from my underpowered BB gun. Sparrows did not fare as well on the lower branches. I was convinced that in their incessant chatter, they communicated danger signals to other birds. There were countless other imaginative games that we enjoyed, just by appreciating what nature had to offer right in our backyards. Those childhood experiences allowed us to sink roots, nurture hope, and, best of all, abet a sense of healthy optimism about life. As remote as Claus Spreckels appeared to be at that stage of our lives, subliminally, it brought us closer to him as self-identified children of Spreckelsville.

We also became "Hawaiians" by virtue of the gifts bestowed by the island and the generosity of the native Hawaiian people. It made us aware and sensitive to the significance of blessings bestowed by native Hawaiian priests. We learned that any place of public use or recognition required formal ceremonial blessings from those priests. Native historical sites became *kapu*, or off-limits, to the public. The restrictions were intended to guard against the desecration of ancient places of worship, sacred repositories of treasured artifacts, and the final resting places of warriors killed during the epic battles prior to the establishment of the Hawaiian Kingdom of Kamehameha. It was also part of native Hawaiian lore to demand a spiritual accountability to *mana*, or the supernatural, in all matters relating to the land. Island legends are full of accounts of fateful consequences suffered by people who knowingly or unknowingly breached that fundamental tenet of Hawaiian lore. The fateful link between spirit and reality was, at times, uncanny.

For example, my uncle and several partners once invested in a pristine stretch of beach property on the island of Molokai with verbal assurances from native Hawaiian friends that it was not sacred land. They were wrong. It was an old battle site where ancient Hawaiian warriors were interred. Within a short period of time, every member of that investment group—all hale and hearty in appearance and seemingly in the prime of their lives— succumbed to illness and passed away. The locals believe that they should have had the land blessed by the *kahunas*. Such experiences became part of the island lore in which we were bred, and it made us believers of powers beyond our understanding. Respect for the land and spirits animating the environment became embedded in soul for all, animate or inanimate, to share on Maui as we grew to know it.

A belief in the sanctity of ritual blessings was reflected even in recreational pursuits. My nephew Joel confided to me about a culturally compelled ritual that he performs prior to a day of fishing at the shore. He begins by offering a simple tribute to the ocean spirits. The offerings may only be contents of a freshly opened can of beer or choice morsels from his lunch bag, but they are offered in genuine humility and gratitude to the ocean spirits for providing a treasure trove of seafood and recreational pleasure—none of which he takes for granted. For the recreational fishermen of old Spreckelsville, on any calm day at the beach, there was nothing more refreshing than the smell of the ocean and the cooling respite that the ocean provided, away from the grinding demands of plantation camp life. For those who fished, at the heart of the relationship between man and sea was an unshakable respect for the power of the sea to take, as well as give, of its vast resources. That too remains as an enduring legacy.

During the Protestant Reformation, the German priest and theologian Martin Luther described the significance of seemingly meaningless and empty rituals, noting, "Even if I knew that tomorrow, the world would go to pieces, I would still plant my apple tree." To the untutored fishermen of Spreckelsville for whom such philosophical musing was out of reach, it all boiled down to common sense and real-life essences that blessedly animated our shared beliefs. Unfortunately, not everyone bought into the idea. But even if they went along just to get along, that was enough.

What of the people who shaped our beliefs in Spreckelsville? Of people who, in and of themselves, were shaped by ironic twists in the fate of immigrants. They, who sacrificed their own dreams of liberation from want so we, their children, could instead prosper in ways unimaginable to them. Perhaps part of the answer lies in a deeply humanistic form of subjectivity that was balanced by a compelling regard for ethical imperatives that could all be traced back to their ancestral heritage. Distilled in pride, it fostered the kind of personal discipline that they passed on to us. Their grasp of irony in their own lives—rich or poor, fair or unfair circumstances, limited or unlimited hope, etc.—were cloaked in a culture of self-effacement and, at times, abject humility. But like so many unsung heroes, they were the real keepers of the faith for us. It allowed down-to-earth pleasures to translate into pieces of a puzzle to confront a far more complex world that lay ahead. As enigmatic as they appeared to the public, they were the real heroes who defined forbearance amid the challenges of plantation life in Spreckelsville, Maui.

The eminent struggle to earn our civil rights in a nationally restrictive political environment, which would lead many of us into liberal political beliefs, actually rested on a bedrock of native conservative values. We were born American, but we were tested by old-world traditions of discipline. The Japanese immigrant parents did not praise us for diligence. It was expected of us. In what we first regarded as acts of brutal insensitivity, they simply raised the bars of expectation. Even as they took hidden pride in our progress, in public they would always refer us as their *tsumaranai* (no-account) children. We learned to understand that, and we learned not just to love our parents but to respect them for what they were trying to do for us. Pride was not about race. It was about our ancestral heritage, which happened to be for our family, Japanese. It paved our way into a polyglot society. It made us appreciate the rich heritage that other ethnic families possessed. It separated economic wealth and status from cultural enrichment. It was a good start to life. It also dispelled some of the dusty images that surrounded the plantation camps.

America back then was not favorably disposed to accepting Asian immigrants as citizens. The anti-Chinese immigration act of 1882 and the anti-Asian immigration act of 1924 both testified to their precarious status in America. But fortunately, the emergence of places such as Spreckelsville had a salutary effect on the lives of the immigrants from Japan by allowing them to extend their identity in time and place to an era of shared happiness and, just as importantly, times of pronounced hardship that tempered their appreciation of life on Maui. To be alive and steeped in hope for themselves and their American-born children was the first line of defense against despair and the potential for self-pity and destructive complaints about discrimination and the vagaries of fate. Having endured dire poverty and humiliations associated with a low station in life, the grinding demands of hard labor, personal deprivation, and daily sacrifice that most of the immigrant labor parents endured for the sake of their children was not lost on our generation. The ashes of memory, even in states of cremation or earthly decomposition, are a valued part of our heritage.

Perhaps a key to an understanding of that heritage lies in the immaculately tended grave sites on Maui, where floral tributes to the deceased express an enduring love and respect for their legacy. Etched in collective memory, each encounter with life that we experienced added to a shared resolve to honor their determination to guide us into adulthood and into lives of mature civic commitment. A powerful component in that phase of growing up was an ingrained determination not to bring shame or disgrace on our families and, in particular, on our parents. That was imparted to us as part of our Japanese heritage. Like the pesky weeds that they laboriously hoed in the fields to protect the sugarcane crops from stunted growth, the first generation of parents tried to weed out resentment and dismay as threats to our own evolution as children of hope. *Gaman*, or enduring forbearance and fortitude, was what they demanded of us, and we understood, even though we didn't understand or speak Japanese that well. Pidgin Japanese was an integral part of pidgin English, and somehow we managed to communicate with and understand each other. Pidgin culture became an enabling feature of plantation culture.

In the current vernacular, the hard knocks of life boiled down to "sucking it up"—a hard notion to propagate today, in an age of abundance where "living within one's means," both financially and ethically, is easily rendered moot by the seductive mantra of crass materialism and greed. For the parents of old Spreckelsville, building character—something that they could demonstrate but not articulate in words—had to precede our entry into a future of enhanced opportunity and material comfort. Outside of the framework of life that Spreckelsville represented, some forgot those lessons. Then, there were the few cynics who chose to ignore those lessons to begin with. "Progress" was relative. But there was always the possibility of redemption in memory—a way that diminishes social status or personal possessions as dominant values. With every return visit to Maui, I used to be struck by the diminished role that social status symbols played in everyday camp life. It provided a refreshing contrast to the dog-eat-dog public lifestyle that pervaded places such as the nation's capital, where I worked for many years. To be sure, high achievement and success of any kind was admired and respected. But back in the plantation camps, people judge others not by what they say or do but by what they are. As Martin Luther King once intoned on the steps of the Lincoln Memorial, it was all about "the content of one's character." Toward that end, what mattered most, the village elders said, in their own inimitable way, was to honor accomplishment—however small or insignificant—as determinants of self-realization. Their hopes for us were not tied to unrealistic beliefs such as, "anyone can become president." That was too lofty. Becoming a salaried office worker would do just fine. Better yet, to become respected school teachers or, for the lucky few, doctors and dentists. Those were deemed to be occupations of real fulfillment because they signified honor and respect gained through honest struggle, not gratuitous entitlement. To be expected, some forgot who they were and where they came from.

When I first applied for summer work at the Maui Pineapple Company, I learned that family connections could land me a cushy office job. My father put a quick stop to that notion. "You start at the bottom as a laborer," he demanded. In private, I initially cursed him for that. But after summer months of back-breaking labor, blistered hands, and an ego shattered by the never-ending demands of screaming foremen, I realized the folly of my own thinking. I emerged from that experience physically tougher and much more sensitive mentally to the demands of honest labor. As usual, my tough and taciturn father offered no explanation for his decision. He didn't have to. In the end, I not only understood; it made my respect and personal regard for him even greater. In later years, it also made me realize the importance of having a father around to aid in the crucial transition from youthful impatience to mature adulthood.

Both realism and Buddhist thought preached acceptance of one's fate in making a go of life. Like the gaming tables in Las Vegas that now beckon all generational groups, it was about playing the odds. Some were destined to win, others to lose—like most of the time if one were to get too reckless. At the most elemental level of life, unregulated risk was regarded as a portent of depression and recession. And the best form of regulation was self-regulation. None of that was drawn from textbooks on economics, which they would not have understood anyway. For most kids of the second generation, the full extent of gambling was shooting craps on blankets spread over hard surfaces such as concrete sidewalks or abandoned platforms, the thrill of which is now being replicated amid the time warp that engulfs the action provided by the gaming tables of the California Hotel in Las Vegas. The lost youth of old men like yours truly, long in tooth, bent bodies, creaky joints, eyes and hearing diminished by old age, now restored to tempered excitability, gamble with undiminished fervor in subliminal tribute to gaming instincts once denied by lives of deprivation. To dismiss the "tackiness" of the California Hotel in comparison to the glitz of the mainstream hotels and casinos on the main strip is to diminish the evocation of the spirit of Hawaiian locals, once deprived by poverty and lack of opportunity, reveling in renewed joy amid an ambience of familiarity enhanced by the gustatory presence of favorites such as miso-yaki butterfish, saimin, oxtail soup, and, yes, even ochazuke and okazu, all served up amid the sound bites of pidgin English. An appreciation of change in recognition of a storied past has a way of making locals appreciative of life even in the slow lane of progress.

The plus side of facing up to the brutal facts of life was that blaming indiscriminate forces and attendant conditions for shortcomings that stood in the way of progress for our generation was viewed as cop-out reasoning. Don't expect free rides, they stressed. Struggle, in the context of plantation life, was about finding ourselves through the rigor of hard work and realistic expectations that eschewed reliance on radical prescriptions to progress. Parents did not fully comprehend the ideological arguments proffered by the prophets of revolution. But growing up in Japan, they became at least vaguely aware of Japanese militarism's pronounced aversion to Western Marxist thought by the time of their departure for Hawaii. In other words, they were quite conservative and apolitical, which kept them on the straight and narrow of traditional Japanese thought until the inevitable advent of ideas such as trade unionism in the islands, which was eventually seen but not totally accepted by the older generation as a bargaining chip for socioeconomic parity. They could understand the restiveness for change among the new generation. But, nevertheless, they were not comfortable with the idea of casting away the paternalistic order and relative stability that plantation life had offered them. Like the traditional Japanese gardens that my parents so revered, the meandering stepping-stones that marked the way through each contour of a minimalist landscape that they cultivated and nurtured to mimic nature, life was supposed to express a preference for nuanced journeys where self-reflection and contemplation railed quietly against haste and impatience. In humble obeisance to nature, they were instinctively drawn to the Socratic adage that a life without contemplation was not worth living.

Loyalty to the plantation bosses with whom many had forged meaningful relationships in the workplace became just as significant as the loyalties that they had learned to forge with leadership figures in Japanese society. It was not a fawning relationship. By nature, they kept their distance. To put it crudely, they "knew their place," not because of their *haole* bosses, but because of a legacy duty propagated by Tokugawa Japan. Respect got its due, as long as it was mutual. In that respect, it was based on an article of faith that somehow, some *haole* bosses would turn out to be benevolent. If that was not to be, then, even in the cane fields, where they toiled, fate was a notion that they could fathom. "*Shikata ga nai*," or "Can't be helped"—win some; lose some.

One unfortunate consequence of early racial stereotyping was a prevailing and mistaken notion among the immigrant workers that all *haoles* were somewhat equal in power and privilege. They were not. Without a doubt, many lower-level *haoles* used race to lord it over vulnerable laborers who didn't know any better. Muscle-flexing bureaucrats of exaggerated power and incompetence were always sources of vexing problems. Those who were victimized had their own myopic view of race—that all *haoles* were, ipso facto, superior in managerial entitlement. Moreover, their conception of legally constituted rights as we know of them today was basically nonexistent.

Unbeknownst to many of those workers, there were social distinctions that separated middle-management *haole* families from the elite class of plantation owners' families. It was the source of the untoward anti-*haole* discrimination that many innocent *haole* kids suffered at the hands of local kids in public schools and playgrounds. Two wrongs did not make a right. But in the long run, the reverse discrimination that those less fortunate *haole* kids endured brought a level of understanding to the local kids that they were like everyone else. The understanding fostered enduring friendships and added both resiliency and strength to the fabric of local culture.

Like any society, the rich and powerful plantation owners bore the onus of envy and resentment that naturally accrued to elites born to social privilege. But, fortunately, there were examples of exceptions to perceived rules of elitism.

Chu Baldwin, the son of the head of HC&S, Frank Baldwin, succeeded in projecting the image of a "good *haole*." He lived in an exclusive beachfront enclave in Spreckelsville. Yet, at an early age, he developed a close relationship with the local Japanese household staff that served his parents. He became fascinated with the Japanese people and their culture and subsequently enrolled in Japanese language classes under Mr. Maehara, a well-known Japanese teacher. With the quiet blessing of his parents, his studies even took him to Japan. He subsequently earned the enduring respect and loyalty of the Japanese and other local immigrant workers who worked for him because of the extra dimension of humanity and understanding that he projected into his style of management.

Chu Baldwin's outreach was hardly the prevailing norm in the thinking that predominated at the apex of plantation management. But it was enough to project the notion, however slight in the total scheme of socialization, that the humanitarian spirit preached by the first generation of missionaries actually existed at the highest social level. That in itself was significant. Significant because throughout the history of the plantation system, there were expressions of conscience—small expressions, linked to a refuge of hope. The American annexation of Hawaii mirrored nineteenth-century nationalism; the ideology of capitalism dominated the race for global market access and political dominance. Racism colored class conflicts that were occurring all over the world. But the force of Christian conscience was not overwhelmed by the hatred of locals. In a place such as Spreckelsville, a seemingly native tropical languor appeared to mitigate the threat of extremist social tendencies. We were flawed on either side of the track. Some *haoles* were recovering racists and vice versa. But among those who refused to budge from their prejudicial ways, most had the good sense to keep their thoughts to themselves.

Immigrant thinking may have been anchored to the ways of old countries, but they were not blind to basic humanitarian gestures and the sincere attempts at outreach represented by people like Chu Baldwin. He was an exceptional member of higher management, and there were many unheralded men like him who made the plantations prosper. Unfortunately, the perception of callous disregard for human dignity openly displayed by many high and mid-managers contributed to the harshness that marked the life and times of the people of the plantation camps.

There were other examples. In the waning days of plantation life in Spreckelsville, Mrs. Frank Baldwin, the unofficial "first lady" of plantation society, used to quietly drive herself to our home to pick up my mother to attend Christian lectures and services arranged by her spiritual adviser, Dr. Joel Goldsmith. There was nothing contrived about their very private relationship. Each knew very well their own "place" in the social order, and both my mother and father—staunchly private people—never told anyone else about those pleasant outings. After the services, the two women would spend a quiet hour or so discussing all matters of mutual interest. My mother, who hosted a popular radio show on cooking, perhaps provided a sounding board for ideas on entertaining, for which Mrs. Baldwin was noted, and my mother probably provided sidelights on local lore, in which Mrs. Baldwin seemed keenly interested. In hindsight, the informal bridging of a pronounced social and cultural gap between the two women may have signaled the beginning of the end of the plantation system in Hawaii. On February 6, 1960, with the passing of Mr. Frank Baldwin, the plantation era virtually ended on Maui. Indeed, soon after, my parents were forced to vacate their home on leased property in Spreckelsville.

Dr. John Burden, my mother's physician, stunned the Japanese community in Haliimaile by introducing himself at a public gathering by speaking completely in Japanese. It turned out that he served in the US Army Military Intelligence Service as a Japanese language officer during

World War II. He went on to become a pillar of society by bridging gaps between the professional world and community concerns. His healing ways extended well beyond the practice of medicine.

Each individual, among many, contributed in his or her own inimitable way to the making of what a noted island sociologist referred to as a "melting pot" of races and cultures—a place where, in the postimmigration era, Barack Obama, the first local *hapa* to become president of the United States of America, received his early education. To be sure, there were imperfections in the Hawaiian social order. But, mercifully, when idealistic illusions collided with reality, gross cynicism did not rule the ways of island accommodation. Suffice it to say, basic human inequalities in fate, capabilities, looks, intelligence, spirituality, etc., were accepted as common denominators of human existence. Racism—including Asian racism and ethnic prejudice—which still exists, began to ebb once people recognized their ephemeral quality and were willing to leave most of that behind. Those who did not remained clueless about the richness of local Hawaiian life, which has the highest rate of intermarriage in the nation.

In a crowded, polyglot island community such as Spreckelsville, where people of so many different races, tastes, and cultures first came together, personal slights, both intended and unintended, were natural occurrences. The very fact that they were "natural" was a saving grace. Racial distinctions were not erased. Instead, they fed on differences to achieve positive distinctiveness. People learned instinctively to recognize their own shortcomings in accommodating themselves to the conundrums of community life. Fisticuffs were quite common (no guns or knives) in settling disputes, but a laid-back, live and let live attitude had a way of ameliorating tensions without escalating into serious ethnic divisions. When the boats disgorged men and women of different hues, cultures, and languages onto the docks of Maui, it was like the landing of Noah's Ark in caricature.

Early on, what the people in the camps experienced along with bosses of all stripes was a realization of common purpose—unequal in perceived goals, but equal in intent and hope for a better future. Bosses and immigrant workers alike became vital participants in common enterprise, which was to assure the prosperity of the sugar industry. In the process bosses and laborers alike managed to learn something of value about each other, and about themselves, as individuals to make places like Spreckelsville a better place to live and work. It was a faint sign of democracy in the making.

Back then, democratization in a plantation society was never intended be "equal," even at home. Until the age of eighteen, when kids left home either to seek their own fortunes, parental rule was autocratic: not democratic. In Spreckelsville, steps toward democratic ideals were etched in patterns of earthbound toil that contract labor entailed. The crude, hand tool-to-soil mode of cultivation that preceded mechanization made human labor indispensable to sugarcane production. By sheer dint of economic toil that fed off of a revered native work ethic, they became something more than mere chattels of disposable worth. Both management and dedicated labor became vital cogs in quest of productivity and profitability. It made capitalism thrive on Hawaiian soil, even during the depression of 1929. Apparently, in the plantation camps, where conditions were already rock-bottom hard, the ripple effect was negligible. Just having a job made all the difference in the world.

The first stage of democratization occurred in accommodation and acculturation to primal notions of self-worth. The recognition of a common set of values relating to productivity fortunately led to a realization of problems that embraced humanitarian needs on all sides of the ethnic and class divides of plantation society. Inequality was endemic to democracy as we first knew it, and as it will always be, as long as democratic ideals are not subverted by flaws in human behavior. That was readily evident in the sugarcane fields, where much of life was played out in Spreckelsville. But once the concept of individual choice and liberty became facts of life, they allowed ethnic, class, and cultural barriers common to immigrant camp life to be breached naturally. Without fanfare, the concept of democracy began to evolve out of our state of nature. On those terms, change was not cataclysmic. It was evolutionary and an unwitting choice for a stable social order over social instability.

As a born islander of jaundiced eye, provincially challenged perspective, and blithe tropically-induced spirit, I am still compelled to regard the multiculturalism in quintessence that I experienced on Maui as the prime source of the democratization that guided us to the American ideal of nationhood.

Among the Japanese in Camp Three, as long as they were left to pursue a relatively unfettered camp life, there was no need to pursue immediate and potentially divisive social causes. Victory was about not losing and discovering, in the process, patience as a virtue integral to the long-term goal of immigrant redemption. Short-term solutions were frowned on, and in the process, hope morphed into muted optimism. An undercurrent of belief was reinforced that good things will someday happen even when it seemed that they were not likely to. For the recalcitrant few, it was like waiting for Godot. But for our generation, it was all about optimism. For the second generation, it provided a launching pad for our own and varied leaps of faith.

Again, it was all about unheralded parents who dreamed and toiled in silence for the sake of their children. It was always about us and not their own self-interest. So much for the children of success who have since gone on to better lives without so much as passing recognition of parents who sacrificed so much for their children's sake.

The Japanese immigrant life that I was most familiar with reflected an attitude of philosophical pragmatism. They brought the ways that worked for them in the old country to the new world of immigrants. However, unwittingly they themselves changed and became agents in the formation of a hybrid local culture. It made their children un-Japanese in outlook, while assuring that the children were at least Japanese enough to understand what was expected of them at a pivotal time of transition to Americanization. Our parents were the agents of change and inclusion into American life. Their English was halting, as was our command of Japanese, but in the ultimate quest of hearts and minds, unstated but heartfelt love and genuine compassion for children trumped the barriers that slowed down our way to inclusion as Americans. That was what the legacy of immigrant childhood in Spreckelsville, Maui, was all about.

CHAPTER 5

Local Nurturing and Education

Pidgin English: "Eh, what school you went?"
Standard English: "Where did you go to school?"

Common sense ruled a child's upbringing in Spreckelsville. But it was common sense rooted in traditional practice, not in modern theory. From gestation to infancy, a child was nurtured in a virtual cocoon of soft love. Cuddling and coddling abounded. It provided a brief window of opportunity to establish the deep human bonding deemed essential to the sustenance of a seamless transition to tough love, wherein a more rigidly disciplined and impersonal phase of childhood development would set in. The proverbial cutting of apron strings between mother and child was inevitably abrupt and traumatic to the child, but there were other children to be taken care of, and rites of passage to a more demanding phase of personal responsibility beckoned. There was no turning back, once tough love replaced soft love. To spoil a child was to waste a life and to concerned immigrant parents facing the challenges of making it in Hawaii, that was not an option. Again, no pain, no gain!

Thus, as they turned from sojourning to settlement in Spreckelsville, they also turned to traditional family values to nurture and guide a new generation of children toward an uncertain future, knowing, yet not fully understanding, how growth would inevitably steer their children away from strict old-world ways to the values of a new and evolving world order. Their foremost parental challenge was to somehow preserve the integrity of the heritage that both parents and children shared as the bedrock of stability for growth and compromise.

They began by turning to what they knew best. They turned to traditional childhood nurturing and educational methods as basic components of childhood development. Initial attempts by plantation management to "divide and conquer" by ethnically segregating the camps may well have actually abetted their integration as a whole into Spreckelsville. It allowed them, as Japanese immigrant parents, some leeway to cultivate and convey a sense of traditional individual obligation to family and community as the basis to transition their children into a more sweeping American tradition of citizenship. Family sanctuaries provided the congenial atmosphere needed to forge compromises between old and new ways of life within the camps of Spreckelsville. It allowed the new generation of children to blend into Hawaiian life without doing violence to local ways. In an enriching multicultural environment, children were somehow able to discover a wider coherence in relating their own individual identity to community living in Hawaii.

From the very beginning, childhood education and nurturing thrived in the privacy of homes where families shared, in muted community confidence, an understanding of the ultimate worth of those lessons to life itself. Lessons of the past allowed the growth of infants to be shaped first and foremost by traditional values before moving on to more local and ultimate American values. The main characters in the drama of immigrant survival and growth were parents, particularly mothers, who, in the vernacular of pidgin, regarded themselves as "nothing," but actually represented "plenty" to their children. In typical Buddhist holistic camber, the means and ends of hope became one and the same in practice, allowing the past to serve the present with equanimity and without the corrosions of self-doubt. It reinforced respect for heritage in defining and expanding the identity of a new generation of children.

The inculcation of fundamental values began in infancy, just as it was back in Japan. Education was directed toward a seamless transition from private to public purpose. Professor Edwin Reischauer once characterized Japanese infancy as a phase of surprising permissiveness and rambunctious brat-like behavior, given the highly structured and controlled image that Japanese adults tended to project in public. What Reischauer detected in the anomaly of childhood behavior was a transitional phase of permissiveness to cushion their transition into the highly regimented ways of the real world. The brief period of unfettered behavior was apparently regarded as therapeutic to child development and, more importantly, crucial to the development of enduring ties of natural love and respect between mother and child. Mothers, with the full support of fathers, played the unheralded but crucially important role of providing the underlying emotional security that their children would need to carry them into adulthood. It made the final cutting of the apron strings doubly traumatic for both mother and child. At that point, it was all about duty. It enshrined love and respect for motherhood in children in ways that institutional care alone could not. It was an early expression of women's liberation, in conscience—of mothers temporarily holding independent sway, in shaping progeny away from the intrusions of a male-dominated society. Their role was unsung, but their impact on families and the children, in particular, was unmistakable.

The intense bonding of mothers to children resulted in what Professors George DeVos and Hiroshi Wagatsuma have referred as a profoundly masochistic relationship that bonded mothers to children. In their analysis, it made "look what you've done to me," a central hedge against bad behavior. To do violence to the intense trust developed between mother and child was unthinkable. What worked in Japan worked in Spreckelsville. The admonition about never bringing shame to one's mother and family was sacrosanct. It also softened the edges of discipline.

In the rough-hewn floors of plantation homes, a variant of native methods on child guidance took root. In the absence of cribs, infants crawled around floors atop patchwork quilts, the size of which determined their range of allowable movement. Under the ever watchful eyes of mothers, an instinctive feel for the limits of movement emerged in infant minds. A child could wander beyond the parameters of the quilt, but the child was always enjoined to return to the fold. Symbolically, the mats not only softened the crawl of infants, they also set limits of allowable movement. In breast-fed comfort of being and the sensation of being strapped to the backs of their mothers whether at work or at leisure, infants gained a universal appreciation for the sense of security that only indulgent mothers could provide. Early toilet training also resulted from an instinctive feel that both parents and children developed for bodily needs. Neither the rigor nor harsh demands of a later life would ever diminish that attachment to motherhood defined by plantation life. The expectations of mothers translated into enhancement of the type of education and discipline expected of their children in schools. Education in the minds of parents was not about bifurcated stages; it was about linkages.

Camp life was what inhabitants willed it to be—stable and orderly—by choice. It could have been otherwise, like a Darwinian struggle for the survival of the fittest. But in spite of hard times, camp life was kept on an even keel by stable families and healthy community instincts that managed to make the quest of education and growth a matter of achievement rather than proffered opportunity. There were no free lunches to be had. That was reality. Dour, dust-blown images of camp life, coupled with the self-effacing demeanor of the immigrants in particular, tended to obscure the underlying zest and capacity for life that actually animated camp life. Stable values allowed parents to set fundamental priorities for their children. They did that by serving as exemplars of duty, quietly expressing a down-to-earth commitment to nurturing and the disciplining of their children as preconditions for civic responsibility. To cynics, camp inhabitants may have seemed like clueless dreamers, staking penny-ante bids on two-bit dreams. But the stakes were higher. "Go for broke" was no mere aphorism. Although success and failure were expected outcomes, they saw in the protracted struggle for a better life, a way to strengthen the inner character of their children. To be realistic was to be steeled in trial by fire. To be disciplined meant to be prepared for life.

Even in caricature as humbled denizens of plantation camp life, there was a veiled pride exuded by parents, which was not lost on their children. In weather-beaten garb, reduced by repeated bar soap, washtub, hand-laundering to a familiar threadbare sheen, they went about life in humility, demonstrating pride in a way of life that eschewed conspicuous consumption and status symbols to which later and more affluent generations would be drawn. An abiding sense of duty steeped in general principles of tradition and culture to which they were once beholden as children in Japan became the source of their own commitment to shape the lives of their children in Hawaii. Their personal limitations were quite evident. But children did not appear to mind. Tough love, even in unspoken form, conquered all. As economically poor as parents were, they were also seen as avatars of a rich cultural tradition, which they relied on to serve as blueprints for the Americanization of their children. In hindsight, they could have become reactionaries, consumed only by devotion to Japanese ways. They could easily have surrendered to "saving face," by blaming self-perceived injustice, such as plantation life, for instance, for their own fate. Fortunately for succeeding generations, they accepted accountability by moving forward instead of just moving on with life. Inertia alone was insufficient cause for progress. They persevered in the only way they knew how—to rally their own families with patience, in a naturalistic quest for a place in a young America not yet well disposed to accept them and their American-born children as full-blown Americans. It was an unwitting quest of liberty in a democracy about which kids were basically clueless in Spreckelsville. That was a fundamental part of local preschool education that solidly grounded children on the basics of family and civic responsibility.

For the first generation of immigrants, the first priority was to prepare their children for adulthood. That meant getting jobs. Getting a job, in their minds, spelled added security for the family and discovery of a sense of place for their Hawaii-born children. The practical effect of settling-in was to link family identity to a community identity; and eventually, into a national American identity. It folded vestiges of a Japanese heritage into a quest of American ideals. A dominant feature of the structured ideals that our parents presented to us was an insistence that children recognize the overriding authority of teachers in schools. Academic discipline was to be an extension of family discipline. Unquestioned authority, though abused by some teachers, was the accepted norm—for good or for bad, just like life itself. Although there were exceptions, some glaring, on the whole, the system worked because old-school teachers also subscribed to the virtues of disciplined methods. Schools produced a generation of trained and adaptable graduates for the Hawaiian job market.

In camp thinking, "making money" was good. Capitalism, whatever it meant—they certainly didn't know what it meant—appeared in practical terms as something decidedly better than life shaped under feudalistic constraints. And the hedge against the danger of greed as the only source of a rich life was embodied in the Confucian dictum, "To profit (unconscionably) is to err." As poor as the people appeared to be, they adhered to a culturally induced moral regard for self-respect over self-interest. Greed was understandable, but as it was pounded into young malleable minds in Japanese language classes, everyone had to stand in line to await their turn. On pain of a swift rap on the knuckles, orderly progression always preempted class privilege. Those of us who watched television accounts of residents responding with order and restraint amid the carnage wrought on them by the tsunami that destroyed the Fukushima nuclear facility in Tohoku were poignantly reminded of the moral high ground that our teachers tried to impress upon our consciousness as kids growing up in remote Spreckelsville. That is what heritage meant to us, even as clueless children. Fortunately the most important parts of our education and nurturing were the moral imperatives that we derived intuitively at a time when struggling in endurance was a major parental fact of life in Spreckelsville. It was all in the nature of things.

After school, Japanese language school provided another link to Japanese ways. Attendance was mandated by parents. Children attended under silent protest since after-school attendance made for long days in class and minimal time for play or just hanging out. But some lessons from that era remain indelible. We remember seeing unruly kids standing at attention before their teachers, enduring slap after head-snapping slap, all the while seething in silent protest. The teachers doubled as martial arts experts, and they were tough as nails. What was instructive about those incidents was that deep down, the young toughs seemed to understand what the teachers had to do to set abiding examples for all of us. There was no dissent; only grudging assent to higher values to curb errant toughs. After classes, upperclassmen were also required to participate in kendo (fencing) classes, where brutally tough standards were set for every student, strong or weak, with one exception—bullies were treated to a special kind of instruction. They were systematically reduced to humiliation with expert displays of bamboo swordsmanship in front of the whole class. It was about gaining humility through a humiliation of childish arrogance. Observing parents stood by in full support of the instructors. It took care of bullying in school. In Japanese school, there was none! There was also no need for PTAs back then.

The key to success, parents emphasized, was self-help. Hard manual labor was to be honored as the touchstone of human exertion—an adjunct to book learning. Honest labor was to be the hands-on way to an understanding of life's demands for progress. Their holistic mantra for life was mind, body, and spirit, with no frills, all wrapped in the symbolic bleach-faded mufti that the workers wore into the fields—practical, protective and totally unassuming in appearance.

My father was an independent businessman, and as an immigrant himself, he believed in the prevailing values of the plantation community. We lived on the outskirts of Camp Three, but our ties to the camp were immutable. Our ties were symbiotic. In socioeconomic terms, we were detached, but culturally we fed off of one another. We were all locals.

The photo studio and photo processing business that my father owned in Spreckelsville allowed him to provide the family with a very comfortable lifestyle. Some archivists have speculated that the huge repository of his photos at the Alexander and Baldwin Museum that document the early and unprecedented boom of the sugar industry indicate that he was probably commissioned by the plantation to document the rise of the sugar industry on Maui. It provided him with regular "access" to both rich and poor families that relied on photographs to record significant family histories. He was a deeply private man of samurai heritage who saw wealth as a practical means to an end—not an end itself. We did not understand the personal anomaly created by his neo-Confucian belief that wealth should not become a source of personal aggrandizement at the expense of ordinary people. But in hindsight, we could also understand that as a pragmatist, he found solace in being able to support his family comfortably on Maui. He made it very plain that he abhorred pampering or conspicuous behavior as personal character traits for his own children. He believed that one could either submit in abject surrender to fate or surmount the forces of fate in affirmation of one's own faith in life—a faith that was enhanced but not rooted primarily in religious belief. Subliminally, he seemed to understand that enlightened social laws could bring order in a state of nature filled with potential for human greed, violence, personal domination, and control. To him, that was human nature in unbridled form and showed that we each owed a personal accountability to life in Spreckelsville. That understanding made us better individuals, capable of eliminating a large part of the fear and loathing that could have undone our integration into life in Spreckelsville and, by extension, into the American way of life. Tough love abetted the conquering of tough times.

Fortunately, tough love enhanced our sense of individual responsibility to family and community in Spreckelsville. Through a very natural process, it somehow facilitated our grasp of individual rights in accommodation with something as basic as majority rule. An understanding of elected government under rule of law as fundamental requirements of a democracy came early with parental prompting. As adults looking back at our heritage, we have come to the realization that under duress of plantation life, tough parental discipline, which many of us bridled against, was necessary. More importantly, it has allowed us to look back in humorous reference to an era with nostalgia rather than bitterness. Parental rule expressed more in deeds than words that life itself, like the cultivation of life-giving soil, which allows us to reap what we sow, was invaluable to civic growth and individual responsibility to that ideal. It made us realize that there was a moral authority to be recognized with humility, to one's own heritage. And in Spreckelsville, anyway, it neutralized a potentially divisive sense of social class resentment. As simple-minded and "country" as that heritage may have appeared to sophisticates, for us, it represents the sense of pride that we still feel in being from Spreckelsville, Maui.

School and school district affiliations reveal a great deal about one's local background. Thus, the question, "Eh, what school you went?" provides a general introduction to one's local identity and roots of social genealogy. The fact that President Barack Obama went to Punahou evokes thoughts such as, "no wonder the guy talk like one *haole*." It facilitates "connection" as locals, particularly when authenticated in pidgin. School identity, wedded to local and personal identity, becomes part of a wider Hawaiian identity, and in ways inexplicable to "outsiders," it abets ethnic and social class integration among locals. It expresses a complex and sensitive probe into one's socioeconomic origins and an appreciation of what that means to our mutual understanding as locals. Like everywhere else, schools tended to reflect the socioeconomic characteristics of their school districts. In the staid confines of plantation life, we seemed to have discovered a common passion for school loyalties that cut across racial, ethnic, and socioeconomic norms. Our accommodation to those differences brought us closer together. To be sure, there were street fights, but not violent ones. Fights were part of the process of accommodation—not seething, everlasting enmity. It allowed us to maintain our private biases and school-based prejudices without doing violence to shared civic responsibilities. Sharing and respecting the basis of that understanding was to be local and part of a wider island culture. To be "us"—rich or poor, followed in the wake of that unstated understanding (after we graduated from school)—otherwise we would not have had school rivalries. Meanwhile, as students, we learned to feel the surge of the crowd madness that animated school loyalties on football days, where "buss um up!" was an overriding sentiment in our understanding of segregated loyalty to school teams.

Our "place" and local identity thus began in Spreckelsville, and we were shaped in pride by what our immigrant parents regarded as the tried and true methods of their forbears. That was what they knew best. But, thankfully, they were not totally dominated by the past. Like the Meiji leadership that looked to produce "new wine in old bottles" to ramp up the modernization of feudal Japan, they adapted their own version of the Japanese "spirit" to Hawaiian ways. In the process, it turned us into budding locals, not Japanese kids.

Some of the mothers tasked with nurturing infant souls were women who as "picture brides," or as partners in arranged marriages, found little conventional romance in the plantation camps. However, many discovered bountiful love and joy with the arrival of babies into their lonely lives. Reality was well-served in a life of coping, and for a generation of children, the impact of tough-love parental guidance was immeasurable.

My mother, who had the good fortune to marry apart from conventional plantation life, reveled, in like fashion, in the same spirit of motherhood that seemed endemic to life in Spreckelsville.

There were two tiers of elementary education in Spreckelsville. Most of the children from the plantation camps went to Spreckelsville School, a regular public school. A select group of students attended Kaunoa School, the only so-called English standard school on Maui. The concept of an English standard school was established in Hawaii under law in 1920 on recommendation of a federal survey team decreeing that attendance at such schools be limited to students capable of speaking and using English correctly. According to authors Cecil K. Dotts and Mildred Sikkema (*Challenging the Status Quo: Public Education in Hawaii, 1840-1890*),

> Although there was evidence that the policy of maintaining the dual system was never deliberately administered in any way to justify it, and the English standard schools did enroll non-Caucasian students, these schools became a symbol of Caucasian disdain for the non-Caucasian population. Segregation protected both the speech and position in the islands' stratified society of those who spoke standard English as their native language. But the great majority of youth in Hawaii were non-Caucasian and were deprived of any intimate contact with their English-language peers throughout their school years—a circumstance which helped to defeat the educational goal of democracy in the schools.[10]

Entry into Kaunoa entailed entrance exams and personal interviews—what some would now regard as actual background checks. At age six, I had no idea what all of this meant. My parents told me to go to Kaunoa School, so I dutifully obeyed. I went to Kaunoa School like all except one of my brothers and sisters. Upon entry, I thought little of the fact that most of my classmates were from affluent Caucasian families. Welcome to the world of naiveté! After school, however, returning to the periphery of the plantation camp scene, I became very aware of my segregated status within the plantation camp system. I was "different" because I went to school with the *haoles*. Many of the kids wanted to "bust me up." I learned why, the hard way. But in the long run, it turned me into a populist, and it made me more compassionate in my attitude toward the underprivileged people of any society.

On a wider plane of social change, a dramatic change occurred when children left ethnically segregated camps such as Camp Three to enter Spreckelsville School. It put children of the plantation camps in intimate contact with a feast of images and languages previously unknown to them. Exploration, even at the most elemental level of plantation life, was as exhilarating as it was bemusing. New sights, sounds, and an insecure grasp of those phenomena elicited tentative retreat into atavistic pose. Amid all that, pidgin English served as the agent of bonding kids caught in mutual ethnic befuddlement, as they faced a phase of classroom emphasis on proper English as the medium of instruction and acculturation.

Subsequent changes in attitude were as dramatic as they were inevitable. At school cafeterias, forks and knives replaced chopsticks, and ketchup became an alternative to soy sauce. Better yet, mix the two, and you got a new array of good-tasting sauce. Spanish rice (paella) replaced fried rice, and potatoes replaced rice as a staple of school lunches. Newly acquired tastes also altered ingrained attitudes. Food channeled into our bodies metabolized not just as waste matter but also as sensory agents for an enduring fascination with new tastes. Food for thought, took on extra dimensions. "Broke the mouth" became part of the lexicon of gustatory joy. Spam musubi turned the much-maligned World War II GI disdain for canned meat into a popular staple for adults and kids alike. Chemistry was enjoined by alchemy as "old country" ways of preparing something as traditional as rice was incorporated into a local fascination for new tastes. We were enjoined by old country values, but steeped as we were in the red dirt culture of plantation life, we became mutants of a new and transforming local democratic order.

The contrasts between Kaunoa School and Spreckelsville School were instructive. On a sliding scale of amenities, Kaunoa School fared better than Spreckelsville School. Kaunoa was situated on a pristine campus setting, partially shielded from full public view from the main highway by sprawling monkeypod trees on one side and a lengthy palm tree-graced driveway on the other for bus and private automobile entry into the school grounds. It was a sanctuary of privilege with green lawns, extensive enough to allow all eight of the classes to be engaged in physical education activities at once without intruding on one another.

In contrast, Spreckelsville School had a visibly utilitarian look to its campus. Its playgrounds were devoid of sprawling lawn carpeting, and the range of playground equipment was bare bones in comparison to Kaunoa. Yet, it would be grossly misleading to conclude that the students were less happy than the students at Kaunoa. What the students lacked in amenities at Spreckelsville, they compensated for with imaginative games and activities. For example, the use of marbles in the invention of games took on new dimensions. Homemade bean bags were used to devise new tests of skill and dexterity among the girls. And games such as "touch base" brought both boys and girls together, for which there was never enough time to enjoy during recess periods. In their own rambunctious way, the kids at Spreckelsville enjoyed more freedom to exercise their imagination than the more structured ways of Kaunoa. Structure, which was so important to our upbringing, also had a way of creating hidden barriers to the integration of a full range of local games.

Laura Yemoto Wical and Gladys Wong both taught at Spreckelsville School in the 1930s. Both were sensitive to the differences that distinguished Kaunoa from Spreckelsville School. And both generously consented to pen intimate accounts of their varied experiences at Spreckelsville. Laura's first assignment was to teach math classes in the morning and gardening in the afternoon. Gardening and home economics, both taught with limited facilities at Spreckelsville, were never, ever, a part of the curriculum at Kaunoa. The reach of John Dewey's educational principles was more in evidence at Spreckelsville School.

Parental responsibility was demanding at both schools. At Spreckelsville, there was virtually no faculty contact with parents. Instead, parents left it to teachers to do whatever it took to instruct and discipline their children. It was a time when mothers regularly toiled in the cane fields beside the menfolk of the plantation camps. They even took their swaddled infants into the fields to nurse and care for them. No babysitters and no day care centers in those days. Other field work mothers stood at the ready to help care for other people's babies whenever needed. A shared appreciation of universal human kindness linked mothers of differing ethnicities. It was a responsibility that they all shared in pidgin. It was in the spirit of shared appreciation of what hardship and deprivation meant for their parents that the children themselves persevered in school. Their social integration was conceived in practice, not contrived for show. In awareness of those circumstances, teachers provided a spirited and deeply empathetic commitment to the education of those children. Like the parents of the children, they too demanded discipline from the children, but according to Laura and Gladys, it was never "mean." Perhaps, because of that, even though there were pockets of mean-spirited people in Spreckelsville, there were no mean streets to contend with in the camps. For teachers such as Laura and Gladys, the most affecting experiences emanated from the students themselves. In their own words, at Spreckelsville, students were exceptionally "good" kids—quiet, orderly, well mannered, and always eager to learn. A rare instance, given today's travails in American education, of untutored children inspiring their tutors to greater heights of love and educational commitment.

The faculty of about six or seven teachers and one principal at Spreckelsville was predominantly locally born and educated. At Kaunoa, the faculty was totally Caucasian and mainland-born. But it would be a mistake to dwell only on the dark side of a storied plantation-dominated past to judge the merits of one school over the other. I, for one, who spent all of my grade school years at Kaunoa, will always look back to those formative years and the innocent friendships cultivated on campus with enduring fondness. Beyond that, we were all free to make what we would of our educational experience at both schools. And whatever our origins and experiences, once we were off campus, we were returned to being locals, which counted for more. More significantly, in high school, I became very aware of how much better the Spreckelsville students were drilled in core subjects such as math, science, and even in English grammar. They didn't speak English like the Kaunoa kids, but their fundamental grasp of grammar was stronger. Moreover, their pidgin was flawless!

Progress from infant nurturing to elementary school education took an abrupt turn as we approached high school education. Parental and family values continued to be the basis of our transition to higher education and modern ways. The prospect of a high school diploma spelled escape from the drudgery of field labor to skill labor. But the legacy of our upbringing was always there, embedded in soul and the constancy of quiet dedication at even the lower rungs of society. As so memorably penned by Elbert Hubbard in *A Message to Garcia*, it is in the unsung, dedicated contributions of ordinary people that society benefits in untold ways.

So far as we know, a successful life here is the best possible preparation for a successful life to come. And while there are no pockets in a shroud, the soul you have, you'd better not barter clean away. The soul you have here will be the soul you have there—else is immortality vain. And whether this soul is "saved" or not will depend upon whether it is worth saving. So the highest wisdom it seems, would be the ambition to succeed in having a soul worth saving.[11]

Fortunately, a balanced ethnic identity, steeped in immigrant family values, was an established trait of most second-generation Japanese Americans arriving for the first time on the campus of Maui High School. Education was, of course, to be counted. But little did the kids from Spreckelsville realize the full implications of the grade school transition into high school. Freshmen initiation rites turned out to be something more than zany rites of passage into a higher stage of education. Most of the freshmen were initially too preoccupied with the new panoply of images that greeted their entry into a fresh stage of education in an idyllic up-country setting. They were "green." Yet, they were transported by a belief in the promises of education as a way to define their individual worth in society. At a time when a college education was not as readily available as it is today, that phase of our life was pivotal to the immediate future of a new generation. Fate, as defined by plantation life, was no longer beyond reach. Suddenly, hope was in the offing.

On a broader front, it also set the tone for our part in creating a more diverse and inclusive local identity on Maui. Coincidentally, adolescent passions, rankled by mysterious changes in our rapidly maturing bodies, made us much more aware of matters as basic as gender attraction and curious ethnic distinctions among our newly discovered peers. In that curious state, perceptions, particularly ethnic perceptions, transcended racism. Suddenly, for example, *"haole"* was no longer an abstraction. How could it be otherwise when a *haole* was seated next to you in class, agonizing as everyone else over subjects as seemingly arcane as math, science, and Latin? Education was thereby elevated to a more humane level of understanding. Within the classroom, the search for an ordering of facts and theory was nuanced by a realization that the struggle for knowledge was universal. Class and caste distinctions were no longer barriers to knowledge. There was no need for childish revolt; there was a need to get better. It turned out to be one of the unheralded achievements of public education on Maui. It prepared us for entry into a rapidly evolving civic culture far removed from the rigidities of plantation social values.

A compelling introduction to an emergent "school spirit" followed, energized by a novel passion for collective identity within the student body. It did nothing to reorder the social order to which we all returned after school. But the wider impact of mutual understanding that cut across class and ethnic divides was unmistakable. The experience muted the hard edges of social stratification common to plantation ideology, and it also established a more humanistic premise for mutual understanding among the students.

It was, as life should be, a fertile experience in the education of a new generation free of the arbitrary restrictions placed on the civil rights of our parents. Education was not just about carefully bounded lesson plans. Life well-lived taught us, in reality, that democracy still is and will be for the foreseeable future a work in progress dependant on human compassion under lawful constraints. Just the exposure, in bemused state of "country kids," to the whys and wherefores of varying lifestyles that formerly divided us reaching a level of understanding somehow initially galvanized around us an inexplicable "school spirit." In quixotic spirit, a spirit of shared appreciation of higher education based on merit and achievement, we were also blessed with the blessedly unfettered joys of growing up on Maui. It made our bonding with Maui High School that much more special. The school suddenly emerged as something more than just a place to get formally educated. Interestingly enough, without design or fanfare, high school became an enduring source of social genealogy for students all over Hawaii. Hence, the significance of the familiar query, "Eh, what school you went?" It was not about college degrees earned in remote locales; it was about high school diplomas earned amid the kindred spirit of locals.

The outbreak of World War II cast a distinct pall over school activities at Maui High School. Wartime restrictions curtailed dances, proms, picnics, and other traditional activities on campus. The end of the war restored the school to renewed exuberance.

Blackouts and curfews became a thing of the past, food rationing expired, and creature comforts began to reappear on store shelves, to the delight of a new generation of bedazzled youths. Money was still tight for plantation families, but the availability of disposable income had crept into the imagination of a generation of youths spurred by consumerism. Through it all, we were blissfully unaware of the changes that the decline of mercantilist commerce was undergoing in Hawaii with the postwar reordering of economic priorities and the looming threat of a world market economy that would bring the rest of the world closer to us. The return of summer employment opportunities in the fields and canneries, all humming with activity, also opened the door to the possibilities of higher education and dreams of more tantalizing lifestyles. Eating habits changed, clothing fads surged, and formerly stunted occupational expectations succumbed to elevated hopes for the future. But the crucial component of that era was the culture of expectations demanded by our immigrant parents, who reminded us that the attainment of dreams comes at a cost to ourselves. We had to earn our way to a better life. And that education and hard work were vital requirements for our growth as citizens.

The possibilities for progress spread beyond the stultifying prospect of work limited to menial agricultural labor. It placed vocational and college education within reach, at a time when the plantations themselves were wrestling with the challenges of increased mechanization and technological transformation to remain competitive in a world poised to challenge the United States on every front of economic competitiveness. To the consternation of plantation managers, who sought continuity based on a supply of cheap labor from generations of immigrant families, the availability of cheap immigrant laborers was destined to decline. Cheap labor, protective tariffs, and mercantilism could no longer sustain the advantages that long served the Hawaiian agricultural sector so well.

For the second generation of immigrant children, hope morphed into opportunity after the war as defense spending, tourism, and a changing world balance in agricultural and technology-driven industries began to supplant sugar and pineapple production as mainstays of the Hawaiian economy. A burgeoning labor movement, which spurred a new awareness of political activity as a foundation for seeking democratic rights, also added to soaring labor and production costs, with fateful consequences for the profitability of agricultural production in Hawaii.

Meanwhile, prevailing socioeconomic trends also impacted on the collective consciousness of a new generation of students. A new galvanizing outlook for the future made high school education, in and of itself, even more relevant to their needs. A renewed commitment to education reinforced an inclusive high school identity that had always been part of the tradition on Maui. Luckily, we also entered a phase of creeping modernization with profound implications for an intuitive understanding of the underlying principles of democracy and personal freedom as conscious reminders of our civic responsibilities. It represented a precursor to the final achievement of statehood. Most importantly, it strengthened our identity with a tradition of excellence in basic education that our schools represented.

"Excellence," as we knew it, was not rooted in genius. It was about a pragmatic, common-sense approach to education that incorporated discipline, repetitive drills, and fundamental belief in the virtue of dedication to the complexities of learning—especially among immigrant kids. Simplicity, wedded to tough love, was the way our teachers guided us to matters of increased complexity, including an understanding of life itself. Whenever the loud tap-tap-tap of a teacher's menacing pointer signaled displeasure at the faltering attention of a student, antennas rose to the occasion. The underlying message was Darwinian. Those who were not fit to survive could go back to working in the cane fields. The brutally unbending ways of some of the teachers were legendary. But the schools produced graduates with superb skills in such practical skills as typing, stenographic arts, carpentry, and mechanical arts that ultimately contributed to the smooth and efficient functioning of commerce on Maui. Efficient cashiers made business hum; clerks saw something of importance even in the drudgery of stocking shelves, and we all profited from the vastly underrated wonders of human efficiency and order. Likewise, the teaching of math, science, Latin, etc., profited from the teachings of men and women who were hardly geniuses but who were basic taskmasters of their trade. As many of us were to learn later in life, attention to fundamental requirements was integral to advancement to higher stages of knowledge. Our ability to grasp those principles and to laugh about our initiation to the hard-bitten disciplinary ways of our teachers—very much like our parents—and our ability to look back and laugh in remembrance of those times still contributes to the bonding of our identity with Maui High School. It was not just any "school," it was "our school," warts and all. In the prevailing age of plastic images and malleable values, those blemishes still count as identifying symbols of allegiance. Being simple-minded country kids, the newfound identity with Maui High School was edifying beyond the bemused wonder of my own mainland-educated children, who find no comparable cause for celebration for school reunions as I do at my Maui High School reunions.

Generational change has altered the depth of such passions, but the bonds of identity associated with high school affiliation live on, more so in celebration of a time of unfettered humanistic care and commitment.

College was about individual self-realization through higher education. High school was about a time of a collective and, therefore, more enduring realization of identity for our class. Perhaps it also had something to do with a time of our entry into puberty—of passions driven by wayward testosterone counts that churned in our bodies during a key period of our lives. Whatever the case may have been, it was a time of inclusion that linked kids from a wide web of communities in up-country areas, plantation camps, and exclusive enclaves of the rich, all coming together on a campus carved out in splendid tropical isolation—away from immediate distractions. Architect-designed, with stucco walls covered in ivy, all encased in rolling manicured lawns and tropical foliage, amid the backdrop of the East Maui Mountains, all enhanced a feeling of community. It was a time of bemused wonder in our growth. Our fancies took us into growing opposite-sex fascination, of stylistic possibilities including fads such as inside-out jeans (denim sewn to expose the back of the material rather than the traditional darker "blue" side of regular blue jeans) for boys, pedal pushers and fetching open toe sandals for girls and a whole host of other trends expressive of shifting horizons. For our class of 1949, the end of World War II heralded unprecedented shifts in the public face of a generation of newly self-assured kids brought on by the seismic changes wrought by World War II. Maui, and indeed all of Hawaii, would never be the same thereafter. Our high school experience broke down barriers to expansive thought and gave us an added awareness of a world far beyond our sandy beaches. The ocean no longer represented a barrier. The challenge of a new world reaffirmed our ties to tradition as a way of moving forward into a future full of unknowns, just like our immigrant parents. The significance of that heritage may not have been part of our awareness, but, most importantly, it was there, buried conclusively in soul We were too preoccupied with the present and only vaguely aware of entering a phase of American democracy to recognize a transition occurring that would transport us to a new era of increased tolerance and promise.

The parade of aged legions of high school alumni members from all over Hawaii, bent on joyful reunion with old classmates, joyfully coursing through the corridors of the California Hotel in Las Vegas, offers ample testimony to the phenomenon of high school spirits still in bloom. To trace the roots of the phenomenon is to hark back to an era when social mobility and thought, once frozen in the stringent conventions of plantation society, was entering a stage of thaw. It was a time of transformation from deprivation and borderline living standards that inexplicably sowed the seeds of pride in whom we were and what we represented, even as immigrant offspring began to emerge in fruition. An alternative course could well have been to succumb to a state of hopelessness and misguided anger at fate's fitful turns. In hindsight, it was a stage in our lives when education, both in family-oriented informality and formal education, placed us in the cusp of liberty, which was so vital to our entry into American democracy. It was a journey that seemed flawed to childlike minds, unmindful of democracy as the most complex but liberating system of governance known to modern man. Our views may have once been stunted by the parsimonious ways in which opportunity was doled out under plantation rule. But to hope is not to brood about hard times. That was the price of democracy earned and not delivered on lacquered trays. Blessedly, it made us stronger and more appreciative of what we now have as citizens. Education both at home and in classrooms provided keys to our future. It was a path to which we were guided by our immigrant parents, not in goose-step arrogance, but in humility. If we are good, it was because they were good to us, through thick and thin.

The system of education and learning propagated by the immigrant generation worked in Spreckelsville. Yet, at school reunions, talk about social or occupational "success" takes a backseat to a rekindling of a spirit of togetherness. It all goes back to happy times that we shared together as kids: no more, no less. Maui High School reunions represent a brief but pleasurable retreat back into simpler, happy times, unfettered by the gnawing responsibilities of daily living to which we are quickly returned.

But looking back in time, Camp Three, Spreckelsville, a tiny plantation camp of no more than a small scattering of families, it was striking to me, as an undergraduate at the University of Hawaii, to note that at least three members of the faculty at the university hailed from Camp Three. They included Alfred Laureta, Sukeyoshi Kushi, and Ralph Kiyosaki; all of whom went on to more distinguished careers. A later representative of Spreckelsville to join the university faculty was Shinye Gima, whose brother Stanley became a well-respected architect who also rose to serve as the president of the American Institute of Architects, Hawaii. That all of these quiet and low-key men emerged to prominence from a small plantation camp is, in hindsight, quite remarkable, given the daunting odds for success that they all faced. For all of those men, immigrant life was not only about unremitting struggle, it was also about hope and opportunity.

The California Hotel in Las Vegas, the chosen gathering place for Hawaiian high school reunions, represents a visually distinct contrast to the glitzy, overpowering images of wealth, glamour, and empowerment symbolized by the fabled "Strip" of Las Vegas. To many islanders, the California Hotel, an art deco link to a bygone era, serves up local food and atmosphere more congenial to an aging generation of islanders. Small is big for octogenarians, who revel in sauntering downstairs with their walkers to pound away at slots or any other games of chance. For many, it is a subliminal encounter with equal chance—something that was lacking earlier in life. Away from home and daily social constraints, it represents a gleeful intervention of opportunity to fight the odds of winning against stacked odds. It is a "Go for Broke" kind of place that even offers *ochazuke* when hunger intrudes. The California Hotel is, in more ways than one, an oasis in a desert where even a small roller can find solace in the company of big rollers. The images are prophetic. To young and old alike, the odds of winning at slots and the crap tables bring renewed awareness of past bouts with fate. Some will be lucky, some not. No big deal! Win or lose, just laugh, and have fun like real locals. In a world of unequal consequences, where rage can be self-defeating, fate ameliorates wayward tendencies. To laugh reflexively at shared twists of fate is to come to terms with life itself. Quiet laughter over small losses or euphoric shouts over jackpots all express the reality of fate.

Years ago, a member of the National Education Association asked me, "What school did you attend in Hawaii?" "Kaunoa School and Maui High School," I replied. His smiling retort was, "Those were notorious schools," which took me aback. Maybe he was alluding to the fact that Kaunoa was English Standard and Maui High operated like one. I don't know, and I didn't care, realizing how far we have come in our own evolution into American democracy. For me, it will always be *Maui No Ka Oi*—the best!

CHAPTER 6

World War II and the Transformation of Spreckelsville

Life is for one generation; a good name is forever.

—Japanese saying

The recognition accorded the men of the 100th Infantry Battalion for their heroism on the battlefields of Europe during World War II produced a turning point in the lives of all Japanese Americans in Hawaii. For the first time since the attack on Pearl Harbor, an army unit, comprised entirely of local Japanese Americans, was allowed to engage in combat alongside other American military units. The men of the 100th were "freed" both literally and figuratively to serve the nation, and the opportunity was not lost on the volunteers, families, and communities alike. For the Japanese immigrant families, the war was about battles to be fought at home and abroad. They were targets of lingering distrust and rank discrimination within the nation at large, and it remained for the men of the 100th to turn those perceptions aside. Their induction into the US Army lifted the stigma of 4C, "enemy aliens"—not to be trusted for service in the US military—off of their backs. It was time, then, to prove themselves on the battlefield, and they did so with displays of remarkable courage and determination.

In combat the 100th Infantry suffered huge casualties, attesting to the willingness of its men to "Go for Broke" for the sake of parents at home, who felt keenly about the conduct of their sons on far-off battlefields. Given their uncertainty as immigrants from an enemy country, they viewed their own responsibility to properly guide their children to civic responsibility and loyalty to America as a moral responsibility that exemplified "true" commitment to patriotism where it counted most—on the battlefield. In a tiny plantation camp such as Spreckelsville where ordinary people of no special human gifts went about life quietly and with humility, common people rose to the challenge of moral conviction by relying on their cultural heritage, ironically Japanese in origin, to impart "culture" to their children to behave and act properly as citizens, a principle that extended to fighting for national cause on battlefields. That was also a part of local culture of obligation to duty that linked home front to battlefront during World War II. Parents hoped and prayed for the conduct of their sons on the battlefields of Europe, and they were not disappointed. The high rate of casualty suffered by the 100th, which led them to be called "The Purple Heart Battalion," was a reflection of joint parent-child commitment. As for the cost of sacrifice, it was like, "no can help eh?" to the locals.

The determination of those young volunteers of the 100th thus mirrored the overwhelmingly support proffered by their immigrant parents, who had long committed themselves to serving the best interests of their American-born children. Their operative slogan, "*Kodomo no tame ni!*" ("For the sake of the children!") suddenly took on an even greater relevance to their responsibilities as parents with the outbreak of World War II. Then it became time for the children to turn to "*Kuni no tame ni,*" or "For the sake of the nation," a familiar theme in Japanese storybooks, which immigrant parents with few other resources relied on to preach the importance of personal loyalty as a core principle of family and civic commitment to the American way of life. The prayers of parents for the safe return of their sons thusly included the fervent hope that their sons would live up to their responsibility to honor America in time of national peril with pride and to a base of identity that ironically had been influenced so heavily by Japanese tradition and culture. For lowly Japanese immigrant parents, it may have taken a village or plantation camp to raise their children, but then the time had come for the nation to shape the national identity of their progeny as they passed into adulthood. And for that, they themselves were ready to step aside and let their children move on to a more fulfilling identity as Americans.

The success of the 100th led to the follow-on formation of the 442nd Regimental Combat Team. The racial composition of the 442nd followed that of the 100th, with the Hawaiian contingent scheduled to be joined by Japanese American volunteers representing various relocation camps scattered around the mainland. The performance of the men of the 442nd turned out to be as distinguished as that of the 100th, and as the decimation of the ranks of the 100th continued, in the summer of 1944, it led to the amalgamation of the two units into the 100th/442nd Regimental Combat

Team. The 100th/442nd went on to achieve a distinguished record that still stands high in the annals of American military history.

One day, over lunch at a nondescript Mexican restaurant in suburban Virginia, where we met regularly in retirement, a distinguished and much-decorated US Army lieutenant general who, as a young officer commanded a unit fighting alongside the 100th/442nd during the Italian Campaign asked me why I thought the Japanese American soldiers fought so hard throughout the war. I replied that I had no overarching theory to offer. But I said that I could offer an account of what I experienced when my brother left to join the first contingent of the 442nd to try to provide some insight into the prevailing psychology of the early generation of immigrant parents and children.

Memories of the day when my older brother departed to join the newly formed 442nd RCT still remain indelible in my own mind. The events of the day began under a clear "Maui" blue sky streaked with billowing white clouds. To me, it was a good omen, since royal blue and white represented the school colors of our beloved Maui High School, to which our loyalty was total. I was sure that the same intense loyalty would carry from the home front to the battlefront for my brother. And just as the Chinese have for centuries referred to high-ceilinged skies as an omen of auspicious occurrence, I felt sure that my brother's attitude as well as all the volunteers was, "The sky's the limit."

The 442nd was a segregated unit, but the men did not regard themselves as victims of racism—far from it. They liked going into battle with their identity intact, particularly as locals. That way, they felt assured that each man's back was always protected. Besides, in their minds, their pride was symbolically about race, private and categorical, and not about racism.

On the day of his departure, as we prepared to say good-bye to my brother Tommy, our initial preoccupation was the sadness of the moment and not the wider implications of our civic duty as citizens to America in time of war, which would emerge sooner than expected.

And it was also not without significance that looking out from the front of our home that day, Mount Haleakala, our revered symbol of island majesty, loomed with crystal-clear clarity in a way that Mount Fuji must have appeared to our ancestors in Japan as their symbol of reverence. But there was a difference. As children, our view of Mount Fuji was captured in imagery—in paintings and photos. Our grasp of Haleakala was tactile. We could gaze at its presence and feel its volcanic essence as we climbed its slopes. But we were never compelled to draw such distinctions in the past. The war changed that. The link in imagery between Haleakala and Fuji was as striking as it was fortuitous, given the line of separation that was about to be clarified for us that day. We were about to gain an understanding of what our Japanese heritage meant to our overriding commitment to America at a critical point in time. It was something that we had understood intuitively but never heard articulated as clearly as it was to us that day by my father. If Japan's attack on Pearl Harbor came as a profound shock to Americans, the reverberations that convulsed the Japanese immigrant community in Spreckelsville were earth-shaking, particularly for the immigrant generation. To have outright hatred thrown into the breach of latent discrimination, particularly on the West Coast, was to invite fears of untold retribution. Fortunately, it was not the case in Hawaii, where cooler heads prevailed.

The day of reckoning for our test of loyalty to America was at hand, and the formation of the 442nd was to prove a major step in the direction of our integration into mainstream America. I was eleven years old at that time, naturally oblivious to anything other than a concern for the safe return of my brother from the war.

I was, therefore, initially stunned by what my father had to say to my brother as he prepared to depart for the induction ceremony in Honolulu. A tough, blunt-spoken man of typically withdrawn persona, my father, rarely given to speech or public displays of emotion, began by saying that he didn't want any of us crying as we prepared to say good-bye to Tommy. My mother wept anyway. He then turned to Tommy, a son more like him in temperament and disposition than any of his six children, and began by saying in essence, "You volunteered to go to war to defend this country. It is the right thing to do because this is your country. Having done so, there is only one thing to keep in mind at all times, which is to perform honorably on the battlefield for our sake, as well as that of your country. For that you must be prepared to die on the battlefield, because that is what your heritage demands. You are an American, but the blood that flows through your veins is Japanese. Never bring shame to your family or to your heritage. This is your responsibility, and if you fail in upholding your duty, don't bother to return home because that would be a disgrace to all of us. Meanwhile, we await your return in honor. Remember that!"

As a child, I was shocked to hear what he was in essence saying, not just to Tommy, but to all of us, that death was the ultimate commitment to country that had to be made in honor of our heritage and family. At a very pivotal juncture in our lives, without any pretense to drama, he taught us what it meant to be Americans of Japanese heritage—a heritage steeped in identity and traditional culture, which we, as Japanese immigrant children, had to obligate ourselves to, in full measure, as Americans. Racially, we were being discriminated against by other Americans, but that was reality in the raw. *Shikata ga nai*! (That can't be helped.) It was assumed that even in diffidence to painfully hard realities, there could be no compromise in pursuit of the true values of both heritage and citizenship. The need for diffidence would inevitably wane with the needs of each passing generation. But those were troubled times, exacerbated by wartime hysteria, and in the minds of the first generation of immigrants, there could be no compromise with vacillating thoughts about ultimate loyalties. In later years, a more bookish Nisei generation would make a philosophic connection between the historic quest of individual liberty and honor articulated by European philosophers like John Locke with a more down-to-earth and pragmatic statement of values about the difficult path to equality and the "pursuit of life, liberty, and the pursuit of happiness" for all immigrants. What a considerably less erudite man like my father was trying to tell us in his own inimitable way was far removed from the vast philosophical reaches of John Locke. He certainly had not ever heard of John Locke. But what he impressed on us was in practical accord with the "social contract" that we, as citizens, owed to America.

A few years later, as I lay on a straw mat in the home of Mr. Uyehara, a plantation field laborer who practiced massage therapy and bone-setting as a sideline in Paia, Maui, I again bore witness to my father's fundamental character as a man of his time. As I prepared mentally to have a severely dislocated knee, bent at an angle, which was by then swollen to twice its regular size in black and blue clotted ugliness, popped back into place, I expected my father to leave the room. But he refused to leave, and he also did not utter any word of sympathy or encouragement as I lay on the floor clutching two iron rings bolted to the wall to prevent me from sliding downward with each jerk of my leg by Mr. Uyehara. I knew that it was to be a test of personal endurance without benefit of painkillers or words of encouragement. But I wanted to spare my father the agony of watching what I was about to undergo. And in an instant, I realized what he meant when he said to us, as we grew up, not to cry in the face of physical pain. Deeply emotional pain was another matter, of course. He looked me straight in the eye, and I understood what he expected of me. Many dumb kids cried anyway, much to the chagrin of other Japanese fathers like him. I nearly fainted in pain as my knee was popped back into place, but I did not cry or scream uncontrollably in his presence. In pidgin, it was, "Shame eh, if I cry." It was also all about *gaman*, or "suck-em-up" endurance, which was what he demanded of us as children. When the ordeal ended, again, he didn't say a word. He didn't have to. I understood. He was thoroughly sensitive to my pain, but as a father, his duty was to get me through the ordeal with some semblance of personal grit. Learning to endure was part of a lesson in duty that had to do with his professed beliefs about self-reliance. Somehow, as his children, we all knew that although he was a man of few words and seldom given to open displays of affection, at heart he was a father who deeply cared about us. As I lay on the floor mat in intense relief, with my knee back in place, I felt a surge of pride in my ever-quiet father, who taught me some of the most enduring lessons of my life. And in a real sense, I gained some inkling of why he told my brother to be prepared to die in service to his country as he departed to join the 442nd.

My brother's induction to the 442nd Combat Team was anything but conventional or orderly. But then again, the times were hardly ordinary, and he himself was not a person of ordinary disposition.

On the day that he first volunteered, he returned from the recruitment office buoyed by the comment of the doctor administering physicals that he represented just the type of physical specimen that they were looking for. He was euphoric. But within days, euphoria turned into extreme disappointment and anger when he learned that due to the overwhelming number of volunteers, the quota had been reached before they got to his number. He would have to wait. He reacted to the news with despair and unrestrained fury. Like a caged animal, he pounded the walls of his room in dire frustration. After one night of that, he embarked on a personal crusade to gain entry into the 442nd Combat Team, no matter what. He knocked on the doors of every recruitment official on Maui, including the provost marshal's office, begging to be allowed to join the first contingent. He even vowed to seek the approval of the island's commanding general. Finally, just one day before the ship embarked from Kahului Harbor, he was allowed to join the Maui contingent of volunteers. He was finally told by the exasperated recruiters that "if you want to go so badly, we can't hold you back." The aforementioned family sendoff of Tommy occurred the day after with the added presence of neighbors, Mrs. Mike Kitagawa and Mrs.

Sam Sato, with little infant Lynn cradled in her arms. It was a memorable occasion and yet very typical of the way life played out for Tommy.

As a child, my mother once took him to a movie that depicted a man strapped to a parachute, soaring down to earth from a high perch. As soon as he got home he fashioned his own parachute and jumped off the roof of our garage, nearly killing himself. My terrified mother could only shake her head and say in understandable exasperation, "That's Tommy, all right."

He would turn out to be a good recruit for the 442nd. He never talked about the war when he returned home. But he once expressed the outrage that he felt when he visited a Japanese internment camp for the first time prior to their first combat deployment to Europe. After his first visit, he and his fellow soldiers from Hawaii decided to go back to their base to collect whatever food and confections that they could find to deliver to the residents of what they regarded as a regular concentration camp, ringed with barbed wire and machine-gun towers turned inward against innocent men, women, and children. His advice to the truck driver on their return was to ignore the guards at the gate and just "Bust through the gate. Who care about court-martial? We going die soon anyway when we go fight overseas. If you no like do dat, lemme drive!"

Such incidents served to allay much of the mutual animosities that initially divided the "Buddhaheads" from Hawaii and the "kotonks" from the mainland. One side spoke pidgin, the other, *haole* English. The difference in the way each side spoke grated on each side. Initially, the cultural divide was huge. The exposure of the Hawaiian nisei to the internment camps was therefore intensely sobering. It made them see the men who grew up on the mainland in another light. Living in Hawaii, few of them were even aware of the existence of such internment camps—no instant television or even radio broadcasts in those days. It broke down many of the barriers of misunderstanding within the 442nd itself. Mutual respect for what each side contributed in bravery and unsung heroism on the battlefields of Europe only added to the mutual respect that all of the men brought to the establishment of the integrity of the 100th/442nd unit. Actions spoke louder than words.

One distinction remains, even to this day—pidgin English. Spoken pidgin, a language that expresses very little, if any fidelity to normal rules of grammar and syntax, and which expresses a penchant for unruly inflexions and pitch carefully tailored to idiomatically inspired speech, remains defiantly 100 percent local. No one just learns it. It has to be experienced emotionally in cadence with the rhythms of the islands to be perceived with the alacrity of locals. Like the loud cackling of mynah birds, the cooing of doves, and the chirping of sparrows, the art of communication imitates the soundings of nature. Pidgin English strums heartstrings while stroking brain waves. My brother, like so many of the men of the 100th/442nd, spoke really good pidgin and average standard English. But then again, they came out of the war speaking better English. Behind their backs, cynics would whisper, "They became more civilized." I, myself, as an incorrigible devotee of pidgin English, would disagree—strenuously!

At his funeral, his tent mate with the 442nd told me about how Tommy used to do some scary things. One day, after a long, physically and emotionally exhausting slog through Italy, they stopped to welcome a contingent of much-needed replacements. Among them were some friends from Spreckelsville, which cheered him up no end. The joyful reunion was short-lived as the inexperienced replacements were immediately placed on guard duty and found killed right in their foxholes the next day. Some were from Spreckelsville. According to his tent-mate, that night, Tommy quietly slipped behind the German lines on his own. Nobody will ever know what his personal vendetta amounted to that night, but he returned safely with the added benefit of a prisoner in tow, probably a guard lying in wait to thwart his return to the American side. His tent mate was amazed but not surprised by the *katakiuchi*, or revenge, that he sought for the death of his friends from Spreckelsville. There, in stark display, was a measure of the extraordinary ties that bound the young men from Spreckelsville. Unconventional? Perhaps! But who am I to judge? I was not there to experience the maelstrom of raw human emotion that was at play.

My brother's conduct was probably against army regulations and certainly over-the-top in derring-do. But to understand his conduct was to understand the ties that bound the men of the 100th/442nd unit. It was what made them such an extraordinary fighting unit. They were true patriots who did not call themselves patriots or succumb to the easy whim of rhetorical "patriotism." They would probably have understood the widely misconstrued statement of the eighteenth-century English essayist and lexicographer Samuel Johnson, who once referred to patriotism "as the last refuge of scoundrels." Johnson directed his ire at "false patriots" who dared to use patriotism for their own "self-interest" without even having been part of the events that truly distinguished the accomplishments of true patriots.

The standard of conduct demanded of Tommy by my father was not unique. It mirrored the role played by virtually all Japanese immigrant fathers charged with sending their sons off to war with the 442nd. It was "in their genes." The phenomenon can be traced to the culture and tradition of close-knit plantation Japanese families and communities. To all family members, going against the grain of acceptable social behavior was "shameful," and it compelled groups of very ordinary men to fight with extraordinary bravery and commitment on the battlefields of Europe. There is a Japanese saying that every family produces one samurai. Tommy was our samurai.

To be sure, discrimination against them persisted. They were ordered to stand aside as lead contingents of American units marched into Rome to mark the liberation of the city, even though they had played a major role in the campaign. "No can help eh!" The 100th/442nd Combat Team became one of the most decorated units in the history of the US Army. But again, the men from Spreckelsville never referred to themselves as heroes or patriots. Their pride was rooted in a very private identity best shared in the privacy of collective soul, which no amount of rhetoric could adequately convey. The depth of emotions that they share in private, even to this day, is something that is theirs and theirs alone, as it well should be. Deep down in the soul of each soldier are buried images of the sheer carnage and brutality inflicted on innocent men, women, and children, as well as enemy soldiers, that cannot be passed off just as a mere "part of warfare." That too is a toll to be accounted for in the excruciating privacy of their thoughts. They are thoughts that only their comrades in combat can really understand. But the fact that the people of Bruyeres, France, a town that they had liberated from German occupation, have regularly made a point to send representatives to annual reunions of the 100th/442nd in Honolulu attests poignantly to the much-reported humanitarian ways in which the men of that unit treated the men, women, and children of that town upon liberation. During one such reunion, a woman who was liberated at Dachau elicited uproarious laughter when she recalled being too petrified to open her eyes to view her liberators. When finally convinced by her fellow prisoners that all was well and that she could open her eyes, she was again gripped in terror to see a man "with no eyes." Apparently, the "Buddhahead" from Hawaii had severe epicanthic folds of eyes that made him look as if he had no eyes when he smiled, and that drove her to delusion. Yet, the fact that she could openly relate an ethnic joke with natural aplomb and humor was an indication of how close she had gotten over the years to the men who rescued her. By then, she understood what *aloha* meant to the locals.

History records the attempts of men such as Adolf Hitler and Mao Tse-tung, just to name a few, to use revolutionary ideological tracts that they authored to rally ordinary soldiers and citizens to national revolutionary causes. But in the end, it appears that it was not high rhetoric but rather the simplified explanations of their ideas conveyed by dedicated German noncoms and Chinese cadres that actually enabled their messages to be carried to the masses. In like manner, for young minds like the boys in Spreckelsville, lessons about duty to country, community, and family were basically taught at home by dedicated parents. Sun Tzu would probably have approved the strategy of making young men understand themselves as well as their enemies—both domestic and foreign—as first principles of duty and conduct on the way to actual combat with enemy forces on distant battlefields.

The subliminal ties between the home front and the war front played a very significant role for the men of the 100th/442nd unit. The *sennin bari*, or "thousand stitch belt" offers a case in point. It was a simple cloth fashioned into a belt containing "one thousand stitches" sewn with care by family members, relatives, and friends, which soldiers fastened around their torsos and wore into combat.

While the belts did little to keep the men out of harm's way, the *sennin bari* provided a transcendent message of care and expected responsibilities to heritage and family tradition over the great divide that physically separated the men from their families. As a child, I remember stitching a Japanese coin on a belt destined for use by my brother in hopes that it would protect him from enemy fire. Old Japanese coins were handy because they had holes in the middle, which made it easier to stitch onto the belt. The symbolic reach of those belts effectively tied faith to fate and soldiers on the battlefield to loved ones at home.

There were also other unheralded roles played by women on the home front. My mother, for example, being one of the few women who spoke both Japanese and English fluently, was prevailed upon by Mr. Ezra Crane, the provost marshal of Maui, to serve as an interpreter whenever he had to personally visit the homes of sons killed in action. Her very first visit to the home of a Gold Star family to report the death of their son tore her apart emotionally. Subsequent encounters to report the deaths of men killed in action to grief-stricken families worsened her state of mind. Being a "volunteer," she soon begged to be relieved of her duties. The equally distraught Ezra Crane, a trusted friend of the locals and my parents, begged her to stay on since he was a *haole* incapable of speaking Japanese or observing the proper rules of etiquette. Out of a sense of duty to friend and country, she reluctantly consented to help him out for the duration of the war. Her only compensation was the gratitude of a few people who were aware of the service that she was contributing for free. After a while, the mere sight of the provost marshal's car pulling into the driveway of homes elicited shrieks of utter grief from aggrieved mothers. My mother never ever got over those incidents. Nor did Ezra Crane, who was equally distraught. After each family visitation, my mother would return home in silence, to prepare dinner for us before retreating to her room to cry behind closed doors, well aware that the next casualty report could very well be that of her own son. And, of course, there were prayers for his safe return. Those were trying times for her.

As children, parental efforts to keep connected with the soldiers provided insights into their innermost character—character traits that I believe actually prevented us from succumbing to the dangers of hopelessly reactionary and fundamentalist tendencies. It has also solidified my belief that wars cannot be won on terms other than the bonding of the home front to the battlefront. The reaches of professional military competence alone cannot expunge the fury of human outrage that sustains the heroism of some and drives others to mental despair. It was not a textbook observation. I learned that at home in Spreckelsville.

The twists of fate that the war brought to Spreckelsville and indeed to all of Maui were manifold. As a child, my own ignorance about what was really going on around the rest of the world, and indeed in the other islands, was a mark of my own provincial outlook on Maui. But to say that is to emphasize the care that parents took to provide children with worry-free daily lives even during the war. Food was rationed, and frozen meat shipped to the islands tasted awful. We may have mistakenly thought that it was ordinary beef that we were eating. But then again it may have been something else, cooked and immersed in lots of gravy and sauces. But somehow everyone made do. Included in the sweep of our wartime experience was our first encounter with the vagaries of "justice," in an evolving democracy.

Federal and local authorities swept into places on Maui, including Spreckelsville, to round up Japanese plantation camp and community leaders suspected of espionage activities. As the only educated and literate men around, they performed such tasks as interpreting immigrant laws and regulations or helping communities to set up local churches and language schools. Some of the men were ordinary laborers. Some had technical skills, including doctors and priests from Japan who were the only ones available to provide community guidance, for which they were not compensated. In other words, they provided an array of public services that would otherwise have been unavailable to immigrant communities such as Spreckelsville. It was all about community self-help. When the war broke out, many of those generous people were summarily arrested and jailed, leaving their own families without means of support. Amid the whispered tones that the immigrants discussed such matters, kids were kept unaware of such matters, unless it just happened within one's own neighborhood.

A case in point was what happened to a friend of the family, Dr. Seiichi Ohata, a sojourner turned resident, who, at twenty-seven years of age, first arrived in Honolulu in 1912 to become a staff physician at the Honolulu Japanese Hospital, now known as the Kuakini Hospital. A switch to private practice soon took him to Lahaina, Wailuku, and even a sabbatical in Japan, for postgraduate studies before he finally settled in Paia, Maui. When the war broke out, he was immediately jailed and shuttled between various internment camps on the mainland. He too was a victim of wartime hysteria and suspicion. His earnings as a private physician catering to ordinary immigrants were modest. And much of the payments to him were in-kind, such as fruits, vegetables, chickens, etc. But as one of the few educated men around, he was naturally depended on by the immigrant community to provide guidance and advice to establish an infrastructure of support for community educational and religious activities. Communal self-help programs developed by people such as Dr. Ohata yielded results that unfortunately warranted the attention of wartime authorities as potential sources of espionage activity.

Dr. Seiichi Ohata was immediately arrested after the attack on Pearl Harbor and jailed in Wailuku as a prisoner of war. In hindsight, he could merely have been a target of opportunity to fill out the ranks of prisoners hurriedly assembled to carry out a POW exchange with Japan in late 1942. All of this took place unbeknownst to his son; Dr. Seiya Ohata was then serving a medical internship at the St. Louis Union Hospital in

Missouri. Understandably alarmed by the sudden turn of events, and on the sympathetic advice of hospital authorities, Seiya Ohata sent appeals all the way to Washington, DC, to prevent his father's deportation to Japan. His appeals fell on deaf ears.

In desperation, the elder Dr. Ohata appealed to his son for help in purchasing some clothing for his involuntary return to Japan. When he was first arrested by federal agents on Maui he was only allowed to take along what he was wearing to the Wailuku jail, plus a toothbrush. As he faced deportation, he was reduced to possession of just his prison garb and a toothbrush! Moreover, immediately upon arrest, all personal property and assets owned by him were frozen under an Alien Property Custodian Act, leaving his wife and seven children with only the barest means of survival. In jail, without recourse to a razor or haircuts, Dr. Ohata, a perennially neat and well-shorn gentleman, was reduced to looking like an Asian caricature of Rip Van Winkle in prison uniform. The utter lack of decency displayed by prison officials toward men such as Dr. Ohata would at least have been understandable had he been duly convicted of espionage or some heinous crime. But he was, by all known accounts, not a criminal or a convicted spy—not by a long shot.

The news that his father was next being sent back to Japan as part of a POW exchange between the United States and Japan compounded the alarm of his son, Dr. Seiya Ohata, a graduate of St. Louis University Medical School in Missouri and soon to be commissioned as a US Army medical doctor. But when his father's appeal for help in purchasing a change of clothes arrived, he was still an intern earning fifteen dollars a month—hardly a princely sum—of which five dollars went to the purchase of stress-relieving cigarettes. Then fate intruded. To this day, he refers to what happened as *Akua Sabe*, translated in local parlance as "only god knows." But then again, it was Christmastime—a time of belief in fabled miracles. In traditional observance of the holiday season, all interns at the St. Louis Hospital were invited to a sumptuous Christmas dinner hosted by the senior medical staff of the hospital. After dinner, everyone retreated to a recreational hall, where doctors and guests gathered around gaming tables that were set up in an adjoining room.

By his own admission, Seiya Ohata was not a gambler, but he knew a little about shooting craps. All he had in his thin wallet was ten dollars, which he staked at one of the tables. When it was his turn to roll the dice, he preceded each roll with silent prayers such as, "Dad needs a suit; dad needs some shirts," etc., etc. Miraculously, by the end of the evening he had amassed a total of $400 in winnings! With suits retailing at around fifty dollars back then, he was able to purchase two suits, shirts, ties, shoes, socks, underwear, etc., for his father. It was a Christmas miracle to remember! Most importantly, it allowed his father to save "face" by returning to Japan properly dressed instead of returning in prison garb. It was to be the last communication with his father until the end of the war. His father spent the duration of the war as a country doctor assigned to a tiny rural village where medical facilities ranged from scant to none. His only mode of transportation was a bicycle for house visits, since there was no hospital or clinic to rely on, and which he abandoned after suffering a stroke that was to leave him partially paralyzed for the rest of his life. In his walking-stick-enabled limp, one could gather only a hint of the depths of personal despair, humiliation, degradation, insult, and loneliness that he endured in silence. Ironically, like his American tormentors, Japanese authorities extended no acts of compassion to him to atone for his plight. His anguish was compounded by worries about the fate of his family, which, fortunately, was then being held together by his unemployable wife and the income of his oldest daughter, a graduate of the University of Hawaii, who was employed as a social worker on Maui. Her pay left little disposable income for anything but daily sustenance.

Meanwhile, problems continued to mount for young Dr. Seiya Ohata, who was inducted into the US Army Medical Corps following his internship. As D-day approached for the Normandy invasion, he was placed on high alert for the invasion of Europe, when he received a frantic message from his sister that the Alien Property custodian was attempting to confiscate their home and property in Paia. They were about to be evicted! Upon hearing of his desperate plight, an equally appalled and sympathetic adjutant in Dr. Ohata's unit immediately called authorities in Washington, DC—the Justice Department included—to try to prevent the Ohata family from being cast out on the streets. It worked temporarily. The Ohata family was allowed to stay in their home.

D-day found Dr. Seiya Ohata on the beaches of Normandy with the 165th Field Hospital, working day and night to tend to the wounded. In the spring of 1945, with the German army in retreat, he was transferred to a combat unit; Company B, Collecting Company, 386th Infantry Regiment, 87th Infantry Division of General Patton's Third Army. They were poised for an attack on Pilsen, Czechoslovakia, when the cease-fire order arrived in May 1945. The war in Europe was over. But not the personal travails of Lieutenant Seiya Ohata, medical officer, United States Army.

Upon return to the States, everyone was granted thirty days' leave to visit families and loved ones at home, prior to redeployment to the Pacific theater of war. That meant all personnel, except Lieutenant Ohata. Leaves were granted only to families within the US Zone of Interior, which did not include Hawaii. Screwed again! He placed another call to Washington. A sympathetic clerk finagled orders for him to travel to Hawaii, employing a technicality that included possible courier duty. What followed was a hitchhiking odyssey through a string of disparate air bases around the country, aided by a treasured travel order and the fact that he was an officer. Along the way, he learned that he needed inoculations to go to the Pacific theater of war. Another obstacle to overcome, but he succeeded by getting all shots at once at a nearby military hospital. Lady Luck again appeared, miraculously. A sympathetic major waiting for transfer to Tripler Hospital, Hawaii, interceded through "connections" to get him into Hickam Air Force Base. There he got a courier flight to Puunene Airfield on Maui. Before turning over the courier document to an awaiting officer, he asked the captain where he was headed. Kokomo, replied the captain. "Great!" replied Seiya because the drive to Kokomo would go through Paia. The one-week odyssey of Lieutenant Ohata to Maui ended at the doorstep of his home, where his overjoyed and stoic mother in an unusual display of emotion hugged him and broke into uncontrollable tears. It was the first time that he had ever seen his mother cry.

When the war finally ended, Dr. Seiya Ohata looked forward to a peaceful and unfettered return to Maui to establish his own private medical practice. But other concerns beckoned, none the least of which was a renewed attempt by the Alien Property custodian to prevent the restoration of the Ohata estate to family ownership. In a display of Torquemadan zeal worthy of an aroused bureaucrat bent on a final inquisition, the ubiquitous Alien Property custodian reappeared at the doorsteps of the Ohata residence to announce the confiscation of all property and assets belonging to the Ohata family. Dr. Ohata had every right to assume that the war was over. It was not!

In the midst of seeking scarce postwar funding to establish his own private practice on Maui, he was then faced with the necessity to divert precious funding to pay for legal assistance to protect the Ohata estate from predatory confiscation. It took several years before the courts finally ruled in favor of the Ohatas. The anguish and high court costs exacted from Dr. Seiya Ohata exceeded all bounds of expectation. But then, the high cost of justice continued unabated. Seiya Ohata next turned to the task of having his father returned to Hawaii. The defeat of Japan had left the elder Dr. Ohata in destitute personal circumstances. He fell between the cracks of Japanese and American government concerns. Neither side was well-disposed to aid him in his plight. There were larger issues to tend to during the occupation of Japan. Who cared that his home was Hawaii; not Japan? His plight was a source of annoying embarrassment to both sides. It was up to Dr. Seya Ohata to grab the bull by its horns. But that was easier said than done because Hawaii was still a territory of the United States and not yet a state. The Territory of Hawaii lacked the political clout of other states of the union. It limited Seiya Ohata's access to political intervention.

Fate again interceded through the good offices of Joseph Farrington, Hawaii's delegate to Congress. Unlike so many others, he listened sympathetically to Dr. Ohata's plea for assistance to return his father to Hawaii. Seiya Ohata was moved by the compassion of delegate Farrington, who could have turned a blind eye, like many others, to his plea. Finally, in 1951, a letter arrived from delegate Farrington informing him that he had indeed succeeded in arranging for the return of his father to Hawaii. When Dr. Seiichi Ohata finally stepped off of the plane on Maui, visibly aged and battered by imprisonment and forced exile, members of his family were overcome with emotion. For the second time in his life, Seiya Ohata saw his mother cry unabashedly. Seiya himself did all he could to suppress the tears that had begun to well up in his own eyes. The odyssey of a man unfairly condemned by fate finally ended with his return to life on Maui.

Although I was not there to witness the event, hearing the story from Dr. Ohata about his father's final return reminded me of what happened to the Arine family on Maui. Reverend Arine, priest of a small Shinto temple in Kahului, was also jailed right after the outbreak of the war, and the temple was summarily dumped at a remote site in Waiehu, leaving his family bare of kitchen or bathroom facilities. The only plumbing was a lone water spigot. With no means of financial support, Mrs. Torako Arine, who eventually succeeded her husband, was left to survive with the support of friends and temple members. She relied on the door-to-door sale of things such as sushi and tofu by-product dishes, which provided just bare sustenance for the family. As she related the story of her early travails to me, I stood transfixed by the depth of her compassion and her total lack of bitterness over what had happened to her deceased husband and surviving family. In characteristically nervous and self-effacingly muffled laughter, which punctuated the telling of her story, and in ways so typical of Japanese immigrants in concealing their emotions, she came closest to what I would regard as the personification of a living angel in our midst. I was moved and humbled beyond words as I bore witness to a level of dignity and self-assurance expressed by Mrs. Arine in ways so rare to our pampered generation.

In the collective sacrifice and heroism of the men of the 100th/442nd Regimental Combat Team, in the patience and endurance displayed by men such as Drs. Seiichi and Seiya Ohata in wanton disregard of their rights, and in the humble but soaring compassion for forgiveness displayed by women such as Mrs. Arine, there was something of the essence of values that the first generation of Japanese immigrant parents in Spreckelsville stood by to be observed for our own generation. Their attitude, which is yet to be fully understood and appreciated by our generation, is not likely to be the standard by which current generations of Japanese Americans will abide as citizens. Nor is it likely that the intolerance that they endured is something that the American public at large would tolerate in this day and age. But it would behoove all Japanese Americans to try to understand that back then grace and humility, driven in large measure by sheer necessity, allowed the first generation of immigrant parents to endure, for our sake, the ravages of inequality and discrimination. In their own imitable way, they preached individual discipline and pride in ourselves to rise above our own vulnerability to such human fallibilities. To them, it was common sense to teach in common sense ways to achieve integration. Unbeknownst to the people of Spreckelsville, integration had taken an ugly turn on the mainland.

On February 19, 1942, President Franklin Roosevelt signed Executive Order 9066, which permitted US military authorities on the West Coast, led most conspicuously by General John DeWitt, to forcibly relocate approximately 110,000 Japanese Americans into so-called "relocation camps." "Concentration camps" would have been a more apt designation. At least two-thirds of the detainees were born in the United States. The men, women, and children herded into those camps were allowed to take only what they could cart on their backs to military barracks-like accommodations hastily constructed in some of the most desolate areas of the American West. The loss of private property and personal possessions forced on the detainees ran into millions of dollars. More importantly, the loss of human dignity inflicted on every man, woman, and child sent to those camps remains incalculable. Adding to the indignity was that every camp was cordoned off by barbed-wire fences topped with guard towers brandished with machine guns pointed inwardly at helpless men, women, and children as if they were hardened criminals. The enforced isolation of the camps apparently served the authorities well. The camps were out of sight and out of mind and situated where there was likely to be little truck with messy debates about the fundamental rights of American citizens. Yet, hundreds of men from those camps volunteered to join the 442nd Regimental Combat Team that was being formed in Hawaii. Their combat record was exemplary. But as those men departed from their respective camps, families and friends were forced to stand behind barbed-wire fences to bid them good-bye.

The loyalty of Japanese Americans to America was clearly in question when the 100th Infantry and the 442nd Regimental Combat Teams were first organized. It was left to the men of the two units, all of whom were volunteers, to respond to questions about their loyalty to America. Their record of achievements and awards earned in combat in the European Theater of Operations speaks for itself. They include:

Unit Awards

Distinguished Unit Citation	7
Meritorious Unit Plaque	2
Army Commendation	1

Major Individual Awards

Medal of Honor	21
Distinguished Service Cross	29
Distinguished Service Medal	1
Silver Star	354
Legion of Merit	17
Soldier's Medal	15
Bronze Star Medal	Over 848

Air Medal	1
Purple Heart Medal	Over 3,600
Army Commendation	36
Division Commendation	87
Military Medal (Great Britain)	1
Croix De Guerre (France)	Over 20
Legion D'Honneur (France)	Over 15
Croce Al Merito Di Guerra (Italy)	2
Medaglia De Bronzo Al Alor Militaire (Italy)	2[12]

Reputedly, the 100th Battalion 442nd Regimental Combat Team is the most decorated unit of its size in the history of the United States military. Add to that the sterling achievements of the Japanese American Military Intelligence Service in the Pacific Theater of Operations, which moved Major General Charles Willoughby to assert that "The Nisei saved countless lives and shortened the war by two years," and one begins to appreciate the wide scope of the Japanese American contribution to the success of US military operations in World War II. And on July 4, 1946, in the crowning event of their return to US soil, President Truman himself stood on the Capitol Ellipse in the driving rain that fell that day to pin the Presidential Unit Citation on the 100th/442nd colors. And the president was moved to say to the men of the unit, "You fought not only the enemy, but you fought prejudice—and you have won." Indeed, their deeds made life infinitely easier for all Japanese Americans to pursue their dreams as citizens of America.

CHAPTER 7

Meeting with Asia

No man is an island, entire of itself; every man is a piece of the
continent.

—John Donne, Devotions XII (1624)

World War II ended on a euphoric note. Assured by battle-scarred
veterans of the 100th/442nd RCT that there would be no more wars for us
young ones to engage in anymore, we embarked on a phase of high school
education that prolonged that euphoria. High school provided us with a
gift of four years of unencumbered pleasure and growth.

But soon after graduation, fate again intervened. America was forced
to enter the Korean War. Desperate mobilization efforts ensued. Hawaii,
being closest to the battle zone, was hit particularly hard. As freshmen at the
University of Hawaii, there were tales bandied about of understaffed army
medics being forced to rely on the recruits themselves to assist in drawing
personal blood samples to speed up their physicals. Harried medics went
down each row of recruits, sticking crude needle devices attached to what
looked like test tubes into the veins of each man. The recruits were then
handed the vials to hold on to with their free hand and ordered to open
and close their fists until sufficient samples of blood trickled into the vials.
Each man was then required to take his own blood samples to a designated
station in the examination room. Some, out of sheer nervousness, dropped
their samples, breaking the test tubes, thereby necessitating a repeat of the
process. Brutal? To be sure, but no one seemed to care besides the recruits
themselves. Wars have a way of bringing on such desperate measures, which
are kept under wraps.

Moreover, many of the recruits were also thrust into battle without
even completing basic training. Local casualty rates were inordinately
high. It was that kind of start to the Korean War in Hawaii. To the credit

of those recruits, it should be noted that in a war that first produced the word "turncoat," referring to those who were brainwashed to cooperate with the enemy, the Territory of Hawaii produced no turncoats. All other states did. For locals unfortunate enough to be captured by the North Koreans and Chinese, being Asian Americans clad in American uniforms made many of them targets of special abuse by their captors. It was a new experience. Asians pointedly discriminating against other Asians added a new dimension to prejudice, which they had generally come to regard as white discrimination against Asians, particularly along the West Coast of the mainland. Discrimination took on a different light for locals encountering equally bemused Korean and Chinese prison guards for the first time.

To locals from plantation camp life sensitized to unwritten rules about not talking down to others to survive and thrive in Hawaiian local culture, the novel experience of having Asian communist cadres "talk down to them" and spouting communist doctrine at them in the complex jargon of Marxism-Leninism—all heavily larded with native Asian accents—was more than a bit rancorous. Part of life in Hawaii was to learn that even the poor and downtrodden respect pride. Locals, raised in plantation adversity to respect the multiethnic and multicultural ways of other immigrants in the islands, found propaganda lectures on racism from guys who were racists themselves naturally grating. Besides, to succumb to enemy propaganda without pride in their own identity meant, "No can go home anymore. My faddah going kick me out of the house, and my muddah going cry." That was a fate worse than death in close-knit communities such as Spreckelsville. Among simple-minded locals, one can imagine them thinking, "Da guys donno nothing but dey talk like we stupid, and we no mo pride. One musubi (rice ball) mo bettah than one bucket full of funny kine propaganda about freedom when we starving and get wounds that they no treat."

In the process, a second generation of Japanese immigrant children was weaned from reflexive groupies into rugged individualists without even realizing it. But the change in behavioral attitude was, as ever, tempered by a lingering sensitivity to local values, once they returned to the islands. The needs of a diverse local culture demanded that. The difference was that the boys of my generation who went off to war returned as men with a far more expansive grasp of what it meant to be not just Asian in America, but Asian

American in Asia as well. Grizzled veterans returned home with greater appreciation of hanging together, even while hanging loose, local style.

When the Korean War broke out, Hawaii was still a territory of America and not a state, meaning that the men who served and died in combat never ever enjoyed the right to exercise their franchise as citizens of America. And while the war opened their eyes to Asia's manifold influences and contradictions, it also put a mirror to themselves as children of Asian immigrants in America. It reaffirmed their ethnic pride in who they were and what they stood for as locals in Hawaii. The experience turned members of the Korean War Veterans of Maui into a far more aware and close-knit group of public-spirited citizens determined to continue to pay civic tribute to a "forgotten war" that bonds their aging ranks to this day.

Warren Nishida, a classmate and war veteran from Kula, remembers regaining consciousness after being hit by enemy fire on the top of a barren hill in Korea. In the eerie stillness of a battlefield laid bare by gunfire, and American units forced into retreat by advancing units of the Chinese People's Volunteers, he lay there, physically paralyzed and unaware of where he was. Riddled by shrapnel from a mortar round which also left one arm nearly severed, he pondered his fate as a solitary survivor left behind in the hasty retreat. Despite his state of paralysis, he managed to roll himself down the hillside like a log and just lay there until he caught sight of Shigeo Otake, his assistant squad leader from Spreckelsville and also a Maui High School classmate coming back through no-man's land to rescue him. As he was being carried to safety, he glanced back at the hill that he had just vacated and saw the entire skyline silhouetted with Chinese troops poised to press their advance. The extraordinary bravery and personal devotion of Shigeo to rescue his buddy, after everyone else had retreated, symbolized the close ties that the kids from Hawaii maintained for each other throughout the Korean War. They looked after each other's backs as an article of local faith. Many hid their wounds during the war, just so they could return to combat with their buddies. It was just one of so many untold stories about locals "taking care of their own kind" in Korea. Like the World War II veterans who preceded them, many used their GI Bill benefits after the war to better educate themselves and make Maui a better place for future generations. That these veterans show up at special occasions wearing matching Korean War veteran T-shirts in tribute to the passing of comrades at funerals may appear "corny" to pseudosophisticated onlookers, but to the vets themselves, it is about remembrances that transcend conventional tributes to fallen comrades.

The war in Korea had another impact on our generation. Our attention was again drawn inexorably back not only to Japan, but to Asia as a whole. Stories about the postwar occupation of Japan increased our familiarity with our Japanese roots, but we knew very little about China and Korea. Moreover, as Hawaiian islanders, we were unaware of what the Asians themselves thought of us. We found out that, generally speaking, Asians from Asia did not think very highly of immigrants who left their countries to make a better life for themselves in America. Ethnocentric attitudes of varying intensity and intent were found to be pervasive in all East Asian countries. It took some harsh encounters with Asians to make local Asian Americans grateful for the kind of polyglot society we built together in Hawaii. Not perfect, by any means, but pretty damn good compared to the rest of our country or even the world. By the same token, we have been equally remiss in being wary of "outsiders" coming in to change Hawaii as we know it, though change is inevitable and may be better for the islands as a whole.

A Chinese friend once confided to me that her first sighting of whites, blacks, and red and blond hair in China was like viewing humanity in "Technicolor" for the first time. A native Korean, who is now a naturalized American citizen, also admitted to me that when he first landed in Hawaii, he was astonished to see so many people of color living in the islands. He admitted that it took a while for him to come to terms with that and pidgin English. Fortunately for us, growing up local and all mixed up was something we never had to think about. It came naturally.

An exposure to the rest of the world also muddled the identities of locally born Asians, which took on many turns—understandable in hindsight, but perplexing when they first occurred. That was borne out during my first visit to Seoul when I inadvertently ran into a classmate from the University of Michigan, who was the bureau chief for the *New York Times*, in Tokyo and Seoul, at that time. We marked our unexpected reunion over a cup of coffee at the hotel restaurant, where we ran into each other with the promise of getting together again the following day. As we approached the cashier's stand at the restaurant to pay for the coffee, I, for one, thought nothing of the lighthearted and animated banter that we were engaged in (in English, of course) amid the predominantly Korean clientele. But for the ever-curious cashier, who was apparently not used to seeing or hearing an Asian talking to an American in like manner, curiosity got the best of her. She asked me, "What are you?" which briefly took me aback. As patiently as possible I proceeded to explain to her that I was a Japanese American born in Hawaii, etc., etc. As I turned to depart, I heard her say to her colleague, in rudimentary Korean, which I understood, "Likely story, the guy is *Chinese!*" To which, my unuttered reaction was, "Oh, well, what's the use?" So much for being Asian American in Asia!

Entry into active duty with the US Air Force further increased my understanding of the real world. Much to my relief, by the time I reported for my induction physical, blood tests were being administered by regular medics!

The most memorable event to occur during my tour of active duty during the tail end of the fighting in Korea came in late March 1954, within a day or so of my twenty-third birthday. On that memorable day, I observed an earth-shaking event that will forever resonate in memory. I was then an inexperienced and naive second lieutenant in the US Air Force about to observe the detonation of a thermonuclear device from a photo aircraft flying eighteen thousand feet above ground zero. We had gotten up at 2:00 a.m. that day for a breakfast of steak and eggs at the officers' mess prior to attending the mission briefing for the day. One statement issued by the briefing officer was unforgettable. We were told that the thermonuclear device that we were about to see detonated within hours would make the atomic bombs dropped on Hiroshima and Nagasaki seem like mere "firecrackers." My own disquieting response to that was, "Holy smokes!" We were then shown a movie clip from a previous nuclear test, which depicted an atomic device placed on a tiny atoll barely sticking out above water level being detonated and blowing a one-mile-deep crater into the ocean floor. And that was like a firecracker compared to what we were about to witness? We could only wonder about what we were in for.

Following the briefing, we rode out to the airstrip on Eniwetok Atoll to begin preparations for the mission. Being on Eniwetok was like being on an aircraft carrier. The island measured about 2.9 miles long and only about several hundred yards wide along many parts of the atoll. The airstrip took up half of the atoll, and the rest was allocated for housing and administrative buildings. Whenever the B-52s stationed there took off with their six turbocharged engines and four jet pusher engines revved up to the max, it almost felt like the world was coming to an end for those sleeping in tents and Quonset huts just below the planes as they gained altitude for their flights on test days. The photo aircrafts on which we flew looked like jerry-rigged vintage World War II cargo planes with doors removed to allow the cameras to be targeted manually at the point of detonation. There were no modern jets with sophisticated camera equipment on Eniwetok back in those days. There were just conventional propeller and a few turbocharge-driven aircraft. The upshot of the matter was that the planes could not be heated or pressurized while we were airborne. The three aircraft, ours at eighteen thousand feet, the second at twenty-seven thousand feet, and the third at thirty-six thousand feet, circled over the target area, flying precise tracks so that the detonation could be photographed simultaneously from three precise angles. In the interval, of about four hours, we froze in our standard tropical uniforms of short-sleeved khaki shirts and khaki shorts. The lack of pressure also made us airsick. Fortunately, the captain of our flight was my roommate, who allowed me to climb into the crew's bunk wearing an oxygen mask until the final countdown to the blast began.

As the final countdown began, we were issued goggles with thick, dark lenses that no man-made light was capable of penetrating, and we were ordered to strap ourselves into our seats and lean forward as far as possible, facing the floor. When the detonation occurred, we were engulfed in light that appeared to be emanating from a million lightbulbs even with our thick goggles on. Seconds later, the shock waves hit our aircraft, rocking everyone in the aircraft like helpless rag dolls. It felt like a huge boulder had crashed against the fuselage of our aircraft. For a brief moment I thought that the aircraft would break apart and send us hurtling into the ocean. Fortunately, the pilots eventually righted the plane and put us back on an even keel before announcing that we could remove our goggles to look at the fallout from the blast. The nuclear cloud and fallout defied description. Everything happened so fast, and we were so thoroughly discombobulated by the enormity of the blast that we were all rendered speechless. We were forcibly delivered to transcendent colors, mind-blowing images, and incomprehensible energy-induced sensations that left us stunned beyond belief. We were reduced to a state of abject humility as we bore witness to man's discovery of another way to unleash nature's inordinate powers for destructive purposes. That was our introduction to the hydrogen bomb and the emerging reality of mutually assured destruction as the cornerstone of Cold War relations.

By the time we finally landed back on Eniwetok, we had somehow managed to collect our thoughts, but we had no idea what was to follow as we returned to Eniwetok. It began to dawn on us that without doors to shield us, we had all been exposed to radioactive fallout from the blast. In rueful reflection of our innocence and sheer ignorance, I, for one, thought nothing of the order for all of us to hit the showers immediately to wash away the radioactive fallout that we had just been exposed to. So we did, giving no thought to the possible impact of radiation exposure to our physical health. Much later, after leaving Eniwetok, I also wondered about the desalinized drinking water being processed on board one of our naval vessels that we imbibed and washed in daily. It must have been okay, since I have lived to a ripe old age to write about the experience.

After returning to Hickam Air Force Base in Hawaii, I learned that a contingent of "Hiroshima Maidens," all of whom had been injured and disfigured when the first atomic bomb was dropped on their city, were due for a stopover at the base before continuing on to the States for medical treatment. On the day of their arrival, I went to the airfield terminal to watch the welcome ceremony from a distance. Upon deplaning, the women gathered alongside the aircraft, outwardly expressing gratitude to their hosts while cheerfully waving miniature Japanese and American flags to the crowd that had gathered to watch the proceedings. Some seemed to be terribly disfigured, but they uniformly appeared to be in good spirits. In typical Japanese fashion, I supposed they kept their innermost feelings buried in thought. Nevertheless, they appeared genuinely grateful to be there.

As I watched the proceedings, I wondered what went through the minds of those women from Hiroshima when they were exposed to the first blast of the atomic bomb. For the doctors and nurses who initially tended to their wounded, there were certainly no precedents to guide them, either medically or psychologically. There were no precedents to guide them through something as terrifyingly destructive as an atomic bomb. It was an imagined conundrum for which I had no answer except to conclude simplistically that that is what warfare is and will always be about. But on that day, as I observed the outward behavior of the "maidens" at Hickam Air Force Base, I thought I detected a glimmer of reconciliation between their grief and a cruel fate that American humanitarian aid was then attempting to rectify on our behalf. There was at least hope that some of their physical scars would finally be excised with the aid of American doctors who were, by then, well aware of the trauma-induced emotional plight of those women. As an American of Japanese heritage, I think I understood that for those women, who had no direct involvement in battle, there was a moral imperative to literally and figuratively "save face" through a form of private reconciliation with what they as individuals had to uphold as women of Japanese heritage. In war and in the aftermath of a war that Japan had lost, the price paid was, tragically, physical and emotional disfigurement. There are times when the most generous acts of reconciliation and forgiveness emerge out of the goodness of ordinary men and women who are somehow compelled to do what is right on behalf of all of us. There was much of that unstated goodness that I thought I detected as part of the ceremony to greet the Hiroshima maidens. As those thoughts coursed through my uncertain state of mind, I was self-consciously embarrassed by my attempt to act the part of a muse on a subject that I was ill-prepared and unqualified to discuss either privately or publicly. It was time to leave and retreat to my room at the bachelor officers' quarters at Hickam Air Force Base.

One footnote deserves mention. On the day of our aforementioned flight to record the detonation of a hydrogen bomb device, unbeknownst to all involved in the test, including the US Navy and Air Force, which had engaged in thorough search exercises to keep the target area free of all traffic, it was discovered, after the fact, that a Japanese fishing boat had blissfully sailed unaware and undetected into the target area, where they got a front-row view of the blast! The fishermen got an even better view than we did. Japan appears to be dogged by annoying bouts of nuclear allergy. The allergy reappeared even more recently when a tsunami destroyed the Fukushima Daiichi nuclear power plant in Sendai. Perhaps it is time for Japan to lead the energy-driven economies of the world to safer and more peaceful uses of nuclear energy.

Over twenty-five years later, when the *Washington Post* reported that no one was really certain what the extent of the power of the unprecedented thermonuclear tests in 1954 would be, I was not surprised. Like other scientific endeavors, results required tests, and we were part of the test. Somehow, it did not bother me that we could have been blown up in the blast or consumed by a massive fireball. The bottom line is that we were not. I was a part of an extraordinary undertaking, and I remain grateful to have been part of the test of a weapon capable of annihilating the entire civilized world should it be unleashed by foolish despots or terrorists. One thought occurred to me as I left the test site in the Marshall Islands. If a nuclear bomb is ever unleashed, I would like to be at the epicenter of the blast and go very quickly. The thought reoccurred to me as I observed the scars of the Hiroshima Maidens.

Prior to my discharge from active duty in the US Air Force, one other significant event occurred fortuitously. I had my first meeting with Japan on a flight to deliver engines and spare parts to Haneda Air Force Base in support of the ongoing war in Korea. The cargo plane, a bulbous C-124, so massive that it seemed to have trouble just executing a turn over the airfield, contained no passenger seats. But there were so-called bucket seats strapped against the cargo hold facing inward, which were spare but comfortable since there was ample space to stretch out. The usual flight time was around ten to twelve hours to Wake Island, where another staging crew awaited to make the rest of the ten-to twelve-hour flight to Haneda Air Force Base.

Driven by curiosity aroused by World War II accounts of the Battle of Wake Island that I had read about as a child, I immediately embarked on a personal tour of the island. I had read that US naval bombardments had attempted to blast every inch of land on the island prior to the American landings. Yet the opposition fire that greeted the invasion force was devastating. What astonished me was that the machine-gun emplacements along the invasion sites were virtually unscathed. The Japanese garrison force had cleverly constructed each of the well-concealed machine-gun nests with thick palm tree logs covered with huge mounds of sand. The tiny, claustrophobic-inducing nests with narrow openings to the lagoons, each with a limited sweep of firepower that adjoining gunners would then extend, provided natural camouflage that was virtually undetectable, even at close range. The camouflage effect was abetted by slight nest overhangs, and apparently the barrels of the machine guns did not extend out of the nests until the invading force was within sight of the beaches. It allowed the gunners to lay down withering bursts of fire at close range with deadly effect. Moreover, short of direct hits, the combination of porous sand and fibrous, shatterproof palm tree logs made the fortifications virtually impervious to long-range bombardment. It was evident that the Japanese command had cleverly used the topographic features and natural resources of the island to their utmost advantage. Wake Island was a "live" island, ringed with live coral. Any attempt to use amphibious landing crafts anywhere other than the lagoons would have resulted in the bottoms of any landing crafts being shredded like mere tin cans. The Japanese defense command therefore concentrated all of their firepower along the lagoons in defense of Wake Island. It was apparent that an understanding of the natural configuration of the Pacific atolls was integral to the intelligence information employed to prepare for defense against the US amphibious landings. As a local, I could appreciate what the adroit use of sand and palm logs made in the Battle of Wake Island.

Finally, on the second leg of the flight to Japan, we arrived over Haneda with the air base completely shrouded in pea-soup-thick fog, necessitating a radar-guided landing. As we circled the airfield to prepare for landing by radar, I was invited to the cockpit by the crew to listen to the instructions being radioed to our pilots by the air traffic control personnel at Haneda. Then, a split second before the landing gear hit the tarmac, it cleared enough to provide a glimpse of the airfield. It was an amazing experience that was repeated with regularity at Haneda at that time of the year. Equally amazing, the first officer that I had to clear through at Haneda was Lieutenant Charles Mounce, who graduated a year before me at Maui High School.

I immediately hitched a ride on a military truck to the officers' billet at the old Tokyo Electric Company building in downtown Tokyo. My first street sensation of Tokyo was a kaleidoscope of images and sounds that was at once cause for bewilderment and intense fascination. Amid the sight of a crush of humanity coursing through the highways and byways of a city intent on recovery, the frenetic pace of urban frenzy, and the cacophonous din of jackhammers, heavy equipment, and motorized conveyances of every conceivable sort, there appeared to be a strange musicality, scored by invisible hand, orchestrated in a symphonic tribute to a metropolis in rebirth. There were no solo performers in evidence to demarcate private and public purpose. There was only a transcendent display of nationalistic pride in play—both mesmerizing and fearsome in implication for the future of a nation that had once succumbed to militarism. To be sure, my seminal impression was that of a "country bumpkin," literally overwhelmed by the dynamism of a nation in recovery.

In a documentary filmed to commemorate a goodwill tour of Japan by the New York Philharmonic Orchestra, Leonard Bernstein was moved to record his impression of a beachside scene of men and women enjoined in animated effort to pull fish nets crammed with the catch of the day to shore. He was moved to characterize the orchestrated performance as a "fugue cantata" played to the sounds and rhythms of human concert. Even if he did not understand Japanese, he could comprehend the bawdy chants that gave voice and syncopation to mutually inspired exertion in naughty challenge to both the men and women there to live up to the nocturnal lovemaking that awaited them at the end of the day. The playful exchange of carnally inspired chants that flowed in unison between the men and women with each tug of the fishnet echoed the challenge of mutual responsibility of fulfillment in both work and play.

Admittedly, for the first time in my life, I was mesmerized by the groundswell of energy that seemingly emanated from the very entrails of a nation in rediscovery. Every great city in the world is said to contain a force that bares its soul. I experienced that force in Tokyo in ways that would, in later years, allow me to savor the experience of trying to grasp the essence of metropolitan greatness, in like matter, in other parts of the world.

One other major impression emerged from the initial encounter with Japan. I came to the unexpected realization that, for good reason, the people of Japan in general regarded me as an "outsider." For the first time in my life, I was pointedly referred to as a *gaijin*, or a foreigner. And ironically, it happened to me in my own ancestral land. It was a sobering and yet, in hindsight, a very understandable phenomenon. From the street hawker attempting to lure customers into a burgeoning cabaret trade, to hosts in crowded entrances to dance halls opened to young students to afford them access to places reserved for American Occupation troops during prime time, I was consistently greeted with "welcome" in English, instead of the "*irrasshai mase!*" (welcome) with which the Japanese patrons were greeted. All of these incidents occurred even though I was dressed in civilian attire and not in uniform.

While discussing my first impression of being a foreigner in Japan, a colleague, who had been born and raised in Japan and educated at Harvard, told me that he could immediately distinguish me as a foreigner in Japan, even if I was stark naked. Indeed, his comment was borne out on the final day of our visit to Helsinki when my wife suggested that we enjoy a sauna at least once before leaving the country. At 6:00 a.m. only a solitary figure was reclining on a bench in the men's sauna at the hotel. His eyes were closed in deep repose, and when I entered he opened just one eye like a one-eyed Jack, and said "gooto morning," to which I replied instinctively, "*ohayo gozaimasu*" which startled him sufficiently to open his other eye. My friend was right. I was stark naked, and the gentleman whom I could also recognize (also stark naked) as being Japanese immediately recognized me as a *gaijin*, even in as far away a place as Helsinki.

I think I also detected another dimension to being a *gaijin* in Japan. It had to do with something as simple as finding one's way around the varied cityscape of Tokyo. Even in our first visit there together, moving about Tokyo appeared to be second nature to my wife, who was born and raised in Beijing. For me, a Japanese American *gaijin*, it took a while to gain my bearings. It was like a clear-eyed Chinese leading a blind-eyed guy with a Japanese name around an unfamiliar city. In our own exploration of the streets of outlying Tokyo, it was she, of Chinese heritage, who instinctively guided me, of Japanese American heritage, in our search to embrace the sights, sounds, and scents of that vibrant metropolis. Our after-dinner strolls out of the Okura Hotel through the cluster of "villages" in urban array that characterizes Tokyo appeared to me to express a kind of primordial Asian way of arranging human habitation. Perhaps it was a reflection of my delusive search for cause where none existed. But I was certain, even naively so, that what was alien to me appeared to me to be elementary to my wife in our pleasant meanderings through the consistently varied and enticing streets of Tokyo.

Certainly, a major factor in my wife's perception of place and direction was the ubiquity of signs posted in Chinese characters (*kanji* in Japanese) which served as instinctive guideposts for her but not for me. She could not pronounce any of the place names since she did not speak Japanese. But the place names, rendered in Chinese characters, quickly registered in her mind in ways that escaped me since my command of Japanese was rudimentary and embarrassingly inadequate in Japan proper. I could not read most of them. If there is such a thing as an Asiatic mode of doing things, born of thousands of years of shared and even contentious civilized existence, it became equally evident that each nation in that web of civilization is distinctive because even copied versions of institutional forms did not and could not include the underlying dynamics that determine the ways in which things are done in closely related cultures. Everybody does things their own way. Well-defined formalities are observed for formal public interactions. Beyond that, cultural distinctions, each unique, hold sway. That's what made me a *gaijin* in Japan. To this day, Asian countries argue and fight to preserve their own identities. It is in recognition of that principle that our own marriage—traditional Chinese married to immigrant Japanese—has survived and thrived in America. Our joint exploration of places such as Tokyo, Kyoto, and Nara brought much of that to light. In Japan, we were guided at all times by instinctive cautionary signs of propriety, just as we mutually heeded in our own accommodation to our successful "mixed marriage." And in Japan, I was happy to be guided around by my savvy, Chinese-born wife, who understood Asia and the underlying dynamic governing my ancestral land better than I did. In the roots of my ignorance was a lesson that many self-described "experts" on Asia would do well to heed: it might keep us from heedlessly rushing into quagmires like the one we sadly encountered in Vietnam.

Also, a bit of irony linked our first joint encounter with Japan. My wife's first encounter with the Japanese came during the Japanese military occupation of Beijing during World War II. To critics of our "mixed marriage," particularly understandable among Chinese purists, it was bad enough that she married a "foreigner," but marrying a "Japanese" was pure idiocy. Nevertheless, our marriage has endured very nicely, and if it is of some consolation to those critics, I am willing to concede that the success of our children is due in large measure to the fact that they were born to a really smart Chinese mother.

Meeting with Japan reinforced my identity as an American. It solidified my attachment to my local Hawaiian roots, and it reinforced my understanding of my ancestral heritage. I have since read hundreds of publications on Japan and Asia in a way that has also expanded my understanding of world history in general. Much of that awareness can be traced to the first footprints that marked my actual presence on Japanese soil. In the process, it strengthened and solidified my commitment to American ideals. The experience linked me even more powerfully to the value of personal discipline that was a precondition for success in immigrant plantation life in Spreckelsville. In the reality of immigrant life, we became aware of the practical utility of a rule of law as a precondition to the exercise of liberty in America even though we were treated unfairly at times. Away from home, it made us listen to and respect our teachers as the guiding principle of education. It saved us from a life of ignorance and self-destructive behavior. For those of us who served in the military, the principle was reinforced in basic training that there is no substitute for rigorous regimentation and head-knocking to achieve discipline.

Finally, the most significant result of my varied encounters with Japan was the aforementioned and unexpected discovery of my father's roots in Japan. He was the main source of the traditional cultural heritage that the family inherited and which my mother carefully nurtured as an integral part of our upbringing. It was not a male-dominant process by fathers as it may have appeared to be. It was also about the low-key role played by mothers that made the transmission of traditional cultural values work. Fathers set standards, but it was left to mothers to sustain an aspired dialogue on who we were and where we came from as children.

Some modernists may be inclined to question the morality of the plantation system and its ultimate impact on immigrant life in Spreckelsville. It probably never even occurred to the elder Japanese immigrants in Spreckelsville to gauge plantation life in those terms. And if they did, we were not privy to their thoughts. For most, their look back at life in Spreckelsville was nostalgic and couched in holistic review. The development of the plantation system was evolutionary. Initially, segregation was a fact of life, and life in general reflected a localized Hobbesian condition of a "brutishness of life" common to the times. Suffice it to say, however, that most revered their relationship to Spreckelsville, warts and all. That is because their identity, in myth and reality remains firmly embedded in the nostalgic and valued privacy of their souls. Like successful marriages that endure in spite of long and stressful bumps in the road, plantation life allowed their generation—a whole generation of some very ordinary men and women—to persevere in hopes of achieving a measure of redemption in sacrifice and search, for a better life for their families and children. We, as their children, could not help but be inspired by their simple and self-effacing nobility of purpose. To analyze the shifting historical tides that engulfed Maui with bitter and justifiable labor disputes, the jarring impact of Pearl Harbor and World War II at our doorsteps, of statehood, and of critical issues that brought an end to the plantations is beyond the ken of this limited discussion. They are issues that require far greater study and scholarly attention. However, it should be noted that of significant importance to our recollection of life in Spreckelsville was the fact that morality was enjoined of children as the goal of family values and not expected of institutions as impersonal as the plantation system. It thereby averted the potentially contentious and divisive issue of abject dependency on the plantation system for moral sustenance. It would have deterred us from an individually more vital spirit of self-reliance. The Japanese immigrant quest of democracy and equality was long and circuitous under a plantation system. But, in the end, the plantation system unwittingly provided doors to opportunity.

Amid the barefoot prints left in the wake of the pitter-patter of children running about our rambling home in Spreckelsville were those of a child who grew up to become the first Asian American state superintendent of education and schools in the United States, another that became a millionaire entrepreneur and author of *Rich Dad, Poor Dad* fame, and a third that was one the few Asian Americans to be elevated to corporate vice presidency at IBM. The legacy of the plantation era was well-served by those men.

And it was, therefore, amid a mélange of nostalgic thoughts that I savored my last visit with my father to the site of our home in Spreckelsville, Maui.

Epilogue

"The soil provides the crop, and the vine shapes the gourd."

—Chinese saying

The first contingent of Japanese contract laborers sailed into Hawaiian waters on foreign carriers held steady by helmsmen well accustomed to the swirling currents and shifting winds long known to Hawaiian navigators. Had they sailed through the buffeting currents of the Molokai Channel, they would have been forewarned of nature's way of causing drifts of fortunes that awaited their arrival in Hawaii. They were wary optimists caught in the throes of a massive effort under way in their homeland to gird for the challenge of Western encroachment. In the swill of steerage accommodations, few of the men and women on board were likely to have been fully aware of the wider implications of their journey to Hawaii. They were part of a reallocation of scarce national resources that was required to affect a massive shift to modernization and self-strengthening to meet Western threats to Japanese hegemony.

A confluence of needs appeared to lead to the first planned sailing of Japanese to Hawaii. There were pressures to balance population growth with domestic resources at home. The timely goodwill visit to Japan by Hawaiian King Kalakaua, just as a period of transition from feudalism to modernization was occurring, allowed the newly installed Meiji leadership to relieve some of the pressure by permitting Japanese workers to migrate to Hawaii on contract. The reciprocal agreement between Hawaii and Japan simultaneously relieved a serious labor shortage being faced by a booming sugar industry in the islands. The contract labor pact worked to the advantage of both monarchies. And most of the men and women venturing abroad were surely incapable of gauging the full sweep of historical change that they were becoming a part of. In their own way, they were unwitting partners in enterprise to promote a bold venture in modern Meiji progressivism tethered to traditional Japanese conservative thinking. Those who ventured abroad to Hawaii for the first time were part of the many-faceted Meiji Reformation that marked a radical departure from the insular policies of the Tokugawa regime that decreed death by execution for anyone caught leaving Japan. In essence, they were pioneers, not just sojourners.

Individually, they ventured abroad for private reasons. There were those who left wary of facing impending impoverishment in an economy strapped for time to effect monumental changes in the domestic order. There were also opportunists in search of wealth and undefined sources of power. But for the most part, they were adventurers, willing to assume risks in a strange new land of which they knew nothing. They were an odd lot, made up of mostly males of varying social backgrounds. As contract laborers, they were sojourners intent on returning to Japan to restake their claim to a place in a New Japan. But as fate would have it, there were few pots of gold, if any, awaiting them at the end of each Hawaiian rainbow as some were led to believe. For reasons as basic as meager savings pegged to subsistence wages, alien laws banning private property ownership, highly circumscribed opportunities for entrepreneurial growth, and, most significantly, demographic shifts in their own midst, wrought by the arrival of picture brides and arranged marriages, plus the welcome arrival of progeny, which produced growing pressures for families to remain in Hawaii. Sojourners eventually became settlers, and settlers became immigrants in Hawaii. Hope and optimism for a return to Japan was transformed into hope and optimism for the sake of a better life for themselves, and in particular for their immigrant children. They knew where they stood and what they themselves represented. It enabled them to face reality, foursquare.

A noted capacity for hard work and humility became hallmarks of their ethnic identity, which paved the way for their integration into island communities such as Spreckelsville. The reality of hard times made them turn to a tradition of *gaman*, or perseverance, as the central tenet of survival and determination in Spreckelsville. More importantly, *gaman*, as a family value, also took root as a community value. It became the price of admission to family, community, and, in the long run, to citizenship in America. In immigrant status, even if it meant turning their cheeks to slurs and insults, it was not to be in obsequious deference to overwhelming odds, but simply in recognition of patience and forbearance as requirements for survival and achievement for long-term goals. A need for self-awareness became a source of community awareness to serve the interests of the entire Japanese community in Spreckelsville. It allowed a disparate group of Japanese immigrants to learn to "stick together" to serve the community as a whole.

Initially, ethnic segregation as the intended goal of preventing the formation of a unified labor movement against the plantation led to divisive ethnic and religious tensions. But in short order, the immigrants themselves began to realize the commonality of problems that they all faced as members of an expanding community. They eventually realized that they all shared the same wariness toward each other that had initially divided them in communities such as Spreckelsville, where Russian, Spanish, Portuguese (Codfish Row), and other similarly described camps once existed. Upon entering public school, children began to play together using the rules of fair play common to all recreational activities, whether it was local games such as "kick-ball" or "touch-base." Ethnic differences began to pale very naturally on playing fields. Parents new to English began to communicate in pidgin English. Soon the exchange of food on special ethnic holidays began to alter the culinary tastes of families. Fresh-baked Portuguese bread, for example, led to returns of gifts such as sushi, chow fun, and myriads of other ethically distinct dishes. It also initiated a local shift to fusion cuisine and the alteration of purely native tastes into local tastes. It spawned a new generation of appreciative "foodies." The progress of integration was natural because the appreciation was mutual and abiding. Like communication in pidgin English, the ingestion of "pidgin cuisine" led to digestions of local ways of doing things.

And in the realm of religion, attitudes took on a Jeffersonian mode of accommodation. At the lowest rungs of plantation camp beliefs, no one cared where or what others worshipped. Blissfully and in averred ignorance, Madam Pele was allowed to share local religious pedestals with other gods. If there was a prevailing local spirit, it was not overwhelmed by religious dogma. Traditional religious beliefs influenced, stabilized, and inspired but did not dominate secular life in Spreckelsville. In Spreckelsville, there was one Catholic church that was predominantly Portuguese in congregation. Protestantism, to which many of the Japanese immigrants were drawn, had its roots in Sunday school activities conducted in vacant plantation home—like structures. There were no Protestant churches, or Buddhist or Shinto temples. They only existed in towns such as Wailuku and Kahului. Plantation camps were "country." Buddhist and Shinto prayers and rituals were observed in private, in front of tiny family altars placed in homes; away from public view, and devoted mostly to ancestor worship. Religious observances were quite important, but individual beliefs tended to be private—in the very nature of ways in which daily activities were pursued in camp life.

Japanese American immigrant children benefited enormously from the disciplined regimen demanded of them by parents who always appeared to demand more of themselves than their children in observing rules of discipline. Their credibility was enhanced by giving of themselves without asking for any credit for themselves. There were exceptions, of course, but deviations from publicly accepted norms only accented the value of the moral compass that they used to guide our development. That part of our education was empathetic. There were no texts. Just real-life street theater played on stages where ordinary people interacted in real time. Bad kids were spanked; anyone caught attempting to cut in line got banished in embarrassment; talking too loud and out of turn drew public rebuke, etc. It shaped communal attitudes, and attitudes shaped the character of the people. Crude? Simplistic? So what? That was the prevailing attitude. It was part of an evolving local culture. In their minds, it provided a natural path to civic responsibility.

Unfortunately, the full range of what they gave us as children was largely taken for granted until it was too late for members of our generation to adequately thank the first generation of immigrants for giving so much of themselves for our sake. As to be expected in a rapidly changing and modernizing world order, many of the succeeding generations ignored their roots and lapsed into unsettling lifestyles dominated by crass materialism and consumerism as central values. But on the whole, one of the most endearing qualities of life on Maui is that much of the old island spirit thrives among families and communities on the island. It can be seen in something as simple as the tenderness with which tiny grandchildren guide their faltering grandparents around, hand in hand, ever aware of their worth to the sustenance of strong family and community ties. Fundamental values persist, not only in replication of storied tradition but also in recognition of shared heritage.

There is no monument to the contributions of Japanese immigrants to life in old Spreckelsville. Nor is there any call for one. Other ethnic immigrants contributed just as much to make Spreckelsville what it was for our generation—a great place to live and mature into adulthood. Immigrant parents sacrificed and endured privations without complaint to allow their hopes to morph into optimism for our generation. Simply put, they gave so we could have. They "swallowed tears" so we would not have to. And by doing so, they allowed our generation to look back with pleasure—not anger—at what was once a wonderful interlude of life in Spreckelsville.

We are therefore left to express the one tribute that is most meaningful to our departed parents. "*Okage sama de!*" or, "We are what we are because of them!" In Japanese lore, much of which is now eroded by passing times, there is no greater tribute that children can transmit in memory to parents of a bygone era. That is what heritage is supposed to mean in Hawaii.

Finally, *Mahalo* and *Aloha Nui Loa* Hawaii, and in particular, Spreckelsville, Maui, USA!—where liberty, individual freedom, and the manifold gifts of American citizenship became part of our civic consciousness in ways that allowed generations of grateful immigrant children to grow up happily as locals—talking pidgin, and speaking English, on the way to becoming unabashedly enchanted Americans.

Notes

1. Paul Wood, "Pineapple Packing Pau," *HAWAII MAGAZINE*, January/February 2008, 19-20.
2. O. A. Bushnell, *The Water of Kane* (Honolulu: University Press of Hawaii, 1980), 105-6.
3. Jacob Adler, *Claus Spreckels: The Sugar King of Hawaii* (Honolulu: Mutual Paperback Series, Tales of the Pacific, 1966).
4. Ibid., Foreword by A. Grove Day, vii.
5. Sun Tzu, *The Art of War* (New York: Chartwell Books), 21. A translated summation of Sun Tzu's statement reads, "We may say that to know yourself and to know your enemy, you will gain victory a hundred times out of a hundred."
6. Kurt Singer, *Mirror, Sword, and Jewel: The Geometry of Japanese Life* (Tokyo, New York, and San Francisco: Kodansha International, 1973), 13.
7. Ibid., 35.
8. Joseph Campbell with Bill Moyers, *The Power of Myth* (New York, London, Toronto, Sydney, Auckland: Doubleday, 1988), xix.
9. Can Lao and Himlee Novas, *Everything You Need to Know about Asian-American History!* (A PLUME Book, USA, 1966), 86.
10. Cecil Dotts and Mildred Sikkema, *Challenging the Status Quo: Public Education in Hawaii, 1840-1980* (Honolulu: Hawaii Education Association, 1994), 105.
11. Elbert Hubbard, A message to Garcia (New York, Penguin Books Ltd, 1899), 21.
12. Courtesy of the Japanese American Veterans Association Archives, Washington, DC.

CPSIA information can be obtained
at www.ICGtesting.com
Printed in the USA
LVHW100359230722
724098LV00001B/61